managing
programmes
of
business
change

A NDBOOK OF THE PRINCIPLES OF PROGRAMME MANAGEMENT

managing
programmes
of
business
change

A HANDBOOK OF THE PRINCIPLES OF PROGRAMME MANAGEMENT

JOHN BARTLETT

BA Hons (Lond), FRGS, LTCL, FAPM(CPM), FRSA

Project Manager Today
P U B L I C A T I O N S

Project Manager Today Publications
Larchdrift Projects Ltd, Unit 12, Moor Place Farm, Plough Lane, Bramshill, Hook, Hampshire RG27 0RF

First published in Great Britain 1998
Second Edition published in Great Britain 2000
Third Edition published in Great Britain 2002
Reprinted with amendments in Great Britain 2005
Fourth Edition published in Great Britain 2006
Fifth Edition published in Great Britain 2010

ISBN 978–1–900391–19–1

A catalogue record for this title is available from the British Library.

Printed and bound in Great Britain
by www.printondemand-worldwide.com

Acknowledgements

The author is grateful to Geoff Reiss for the provision of the core material for the Bibliography and for acting as a quality assurer. Thanks also go to Roger Cully, formerly Programme Office Manager of the Inland Revenue Self-Assessment Programme, for the provision of the SA Programme Completion Report and for permission to include material from the programme. The photograph on page 92 is reproduced by permission of the Inland Revenue.

The author also acknowledges the assistance of The British Library for the provision of information relating to its programme, particularly the book 'The British Library and The St Pancras Building', by Sir Anthony Kenny (ISBN 0-7123-0395-2). Also to NCR Limited for allowing the publication of material relating to its Preparation for the Euro programme.

Contents

About this book

Chapter 1 deals with the concept of programme management and offers a working definition. It also tackles the difficult decision whether to implement change as a stand-alone project or programme of projects.

Chapter 2 places programme management in the context of corporate change, and shows its applicability to today's business requirements.

Chapter 3 demonstrates how change can move from idea to programme. It offers a structured approach along a path from Business Strategy to Change Blueprint to Programme Feasibility to Programme Design.

Chapter 4 continues the work of Programme Design, showing how a programme can be organised. Suggested roles and their relationships are given, together with their placement in an organisation chart.

Chapter 5 focuses on the organisational concept of the Programme Office. It includes typical roles, job descriptions and functional activities.

Chapter 6 concentrates on managing risk. It covers the complete programme lifespan, from designing and organising a programme to its ongoing management, and examines the things that can go wrong in a programme, as well as offering eight key things to get right. Advice on establishing risk management for a programme and performing risk analysis is also given.

Chapter 7 concentrates on benefits management. It also covers the complete programme lifespan, offering advice on identifying benefits to managing their achievement.

Chapter 8 shares some of the author's experience in using soft systems thinking to create change blueprints, benefits maps and risk pathways for business change programmes.

Chapter 9 deals with how a programme is governed by the Programme Executive and Steering Group. It shows the information requirements for each of these groups, including the Programme Director, and how a Programme Office can manage each requirement.

Chapter 10 concludes the book and provides information for further study.

A *Programme management bibliography* contains books, journals and conference papers. Obscure or difficult to obtain seminar and conference papers have been omitted. The Association for Project Management may be able to assist with finding papers published in *Project* magazine, the *International Journal of Project Management* and the proceedings of IPMA affiliated onferences. For journal, conference and seminar material produced by *Project Manager Today* contact the publisher.

A Glossary follows showing common project, programme and change management terms together with the chapters in which they appear.

An Index completes the book.

$p$reface

In the light of well-advertised programme failures, company managers and directors are continually looking for proven techniques for tackling large programmes of business and information technology (IT) change.

This book aims to fulfil that need. It complements existing programme methodologies and frameworks by providing detailed knowledge of the essential programme management elements, and sets out the principles required for good practice. The characteristics of programmes are discussed together with appropriate management techniques.

The material is drawn from my practical business experience in the fields of project and programme management, which include NCR's *Implementation of the Euro Programme* and the *NHS National Programme for IT*. It is based on concepts from various methods, which I have honed in practice, including the guidance published by the UK Office of Government Commerce (OGC) entitled *Managing Successful Programmes.*

For all those implementing or playing a role in a business programme, from executive management downwards, this book sets out the practical steps that can lead to success.

John Bartlett

About the author

John Bartlett has enjoyed a long career in project and programme management, commencing with IBM UK Ltd, where he consulted to clients in a range of industries in both the private and public sectors. He later held the post of Head of Project Management for the UK and Ireland at DMR Consulting Group, where he was responsible for developing a project management capability and assisting clients with the specification and management of business and IT change. He latterly held the posts of Director of Technology Services and Director in the European Programme Office at NCR Ltd. Here, he directed the implementation of the Euro programme. More recently, he has been an independent consultant in business change, and in 2004 was instrumental in organising the Fujitsu Consortium's part of the massive NHS National Programme for IT.

He is a Fellow of the Association for Project Management; an APM Certificated Project Manager; a Fellow of the Royal Society for the Encouragement of Arts, Manufactures and Commerce; and a Licentiate of Trinity College of Music, London. His published books and papers, which include *Managing Risk for Projects and Programmes* (2002), *Managing Programmes of Business Change* (1998, 2000, 2002, 2006), *Management of Programme Risk* (pub. TSO, 1995) and *Right First and Every Time* (2005), are testimony to his contribution to the development of current risk, programme and quality management thinking. He also has a strong interest in music and the arts, and has published two reference books on decorative ceramics.

Chapter 1

*i*ntroduction

Programme management is fast becoming an important management technique in the world of business change. Since the publication of the first serious book on programme management in 1994, (*A Guide to Programme Management*, CCTA, UK), interest in the subject has burgeoned. Subsequent editions of this book, published as *Managing Successful Programmes,* have maintained the demand for further knowledge. However, programme management still has a long way to go before catching up with its related discipline, project management, even though it may share some of the latter's management techniques.

The need to have a structured approach in order to manage business change has been an increasing requirement of blue chip enterprises, but not until the 1990s was a solution seriously looked for. The 1990s saw mergers and acquisitions on an unprecedented scale, and businesses had to embark on wholesale restructuring following the worldwide recessions of the early part of the decade. The wholesale change has continued into the early 21st. century with further large-scale mergers and acquisitions and business recessions. To manage change of this magnitude, programme management has become the de facto approach, even though, in its embryonic state, there are still arguments over its essential elements. The main principles, however, are fairly well established, and debate over the next few years will surely centre on pinning down the terminology and fine tuning its elements.

The main area of debate has been the differences between programme management and project management. This is where many people find difficulty, particularly in making the important decision whether a desired business change should be structured as a programme or a project. The definitions given later in this chapter set out the essential differences, and should leave the reader in no doubt about how to make the right decision.

It is ironic that the first real test of programme management in recent years came not from the influences mentioned earlier but from a seemingly innocuous decision made years ago by computer programmers to code years using only two digits. This Year 2000 problem, or the failure of many computers and computer programs to properly recognise dates in the year 2000 and beyond, had major implications for business and government. The test was significant for programme management because the problem affected every part of a company's organisation, and enormous resources had to be marshalled to tackle it.

Programme management was recognised as a key approach for solving this problem, and Year 2000 programmes were implemented on an unprecedented scale worldwide. There are many who would decry the enormous cost and effort involved in solving the Year 2000 problem, but millions of lines of code were changed, and the fact that the millennium new year passed without any serious computing incident bears testimony to the effort and cost expended.

The lessons learned from Year 2000 have had to be applied with equal vigour to other examples of whole company change, such as preparation for the Euro, customer relationship management (CRM) programmes, e-commerce programmes, mergers and acquisitions and enterprise resource management (ERM) programmes. While Year 2000 programmes were driven from technical problems, these programmes are being undertaken for business or legislative reasons, and reflect the diverse changes now regularly occurring worldwide. E-commerce, for example, is challenging the way companies trade and operate. Much of this change can only be tackled at a programme level.

Undoubtedly, the first decades of the millennium will see further large-scale business change, as companies fight for product and service supremacy, increased market-share and increased profitability. Programme management will have to become a much more sophisticated discipline in order to tackle the complexities of this accelerating change. Forces such as the Internet, electronic commerce and Smart cards will significantly change working habits and patterns, and management techniques will have to cater for these revolutionary changes.

There is no programme management methodology currently, as there are project management methodologies. There are only frameworks that act as guidance for good practice. This book is one of these. Its guidance is taken from tough practice, and there is nothing mentioned in terms of technique that has not been tried successfully.

What defines a programme?

Several definitions of a programme exist currently, each offering a differing perspective on a similar theme, ie, that a programme is a collection of vehicles for change, designed to achieve a strategic objective. *Programme management* is the approach taken to manage a programme, which may comprise the employment of a management method or selection of appropriate management techniques.

In many definitions, *vehicles for change* is often substituted by *projects*, but in the author's experience, projects are not the only vehicles for change. Incremental or operational change can be accomplished which does not require the discipline of a project to carry it through. Such change can still validly be part of a programme, particularly if it is undertaken as a preparatory measure, like an investigation or questionnaire survey.

The word *collection* is important, since, in a programme, the vehicles for change are often not physically related to each other, unlike sub-projects within a project. For example, a project to fit out a new warehouse and an investigation into the number of customers with an "A" credit rating are not obviously related vehicles for change, but they could be parts of an overall business programme to diversify product supply. Thus, although each vehicle may be physically different, it relates to the programme through its contribution to the overall strategic objective. Also, projects within a programme often depend on synergy. One project might only be successful if other projects complete in a certain way. A programme is an ideal vehicle for the management of such synergy.

In a project, sub-projects are traditionally formed out of discrete pieces of work from a work-breakdown-structure. They are typically related to the design, development and implementation phases of a project and not just the end objective. Thus, a project to fit out a new warehouse may contain sub-projects such as trunking and cabling, fitments construction, warehouse operations and goods inwards handling. These are clearly related to each other throughout various phases of the project's lifespan. The warehouse fit-out project, however, is not related in the same way to other projects or change vehicles in the product supply programme, as it is to its sub-projects. A project to implement an ordering process via the Internet, for example, is quite different. Both projects, though, if implemented, will contribute to the overall programme's strategic objective.

Most definitions agree on the *business objective* goal, whether the actual words used are strategic business objective, strategy, goal or aim. Programme management is at a state currently where definitions are still somewhat fluid. This is no surprise as even a more mature discipline such as project management may have many definitions.

Programmes exhibit certain characteristics, which some people like to include as part of the definition. These relate often to the longevity of programmes or their position within a company. It is true that programmes tend to be longer in duration than projects, and may, in fact, be self perpetuating or ongoing. Certainly, they tend to have a higher focus within a company because they are strategic and do not usually apply below departmental level. In my opinion, however, any definition of *programme* should be kept as simple as possible. I favour the definition of a business programme as "a collection of

Project	Programme	Chapter
Focus is on a single objective, usually non-strategic	Focus is on a business strategy, always strategic	1,2
The change which a project seeks to bring about is narrow	The change which a project seeks to bring about is wide-ranging	1,2
Benefits are delivered through a single undertaking and accrue usually only after its completion	Benefits are delivered incrementally by projects and other change vehicles during the lifespan of the programme	7
Main deliverables tend to be few	Main deliverables tend to be many	3
Timescale is usually rigidly defined	Timescale is loosely defined, with some exceptions	2,3
Scope changes are managed as exceptional events	A programme is defined for scope changes	1,2
Sub-projects are related to project outcome and to themselves	Projects and other change vehicles are related to project outcome, but may be otherwise unrelated	1
A project is organised usually into sponsor, project manager, sub-project managers and team	A programme is organised usually into programme manager, executive team and project managers	4
A project is applicable to any level of an organisation	A programme is usually applicable to departmental level or higher levels of an organisation	2

Table 1 Main differences between project and programme

vehicles for change, designed to achieve a strategic business objective".

Table 1 summarises the main differences between a project and a programme, which are covered in detail under the relevant chapters in this book.

Whereas projects tend to have a singular focus and deliver to specific objectives, programmes tend to take a wider view and deliver a multiplicity of objectives towards the achievement of a business strategy. The construction of the Channel Tunnel, linking England to France, for example, might have been conceived by some as a large project, but in reality it was a major programme of change. The tunnel has been operational for several years and many of the projects have been completed, but the original programme only completed with the opening of the high-speed line from St. Pancras. Had the strategy been conceived originally as a programme and not just as individual projects, the important sponsorship, funding and economies of scale might have been better achieved. A programme could also have stayed in place to accommodate further enhancements in an evolving strategy. Piecemeal development is always more costly in the long term.

Another key difference between a project and programme relates to the achievement of benefits. Benefits are achieved during the life of a programme, as completing projects are decommissioned and new ones commissioned. In a project, benefits only usually accrue once the project has completed, and after the project team has been disbanded few organisations seriously put into practice a benefits management regime. A programme, however, is an ideal vehicle for monitoring the achievement of benefits. If a particular completed project did not achieve its desired outcome after a period of time, the programme can commission another project to take corrective action.

Throughout the following chapters these key differences between project and programme will be exemplified. However, understanding the differences is one thing. Being able to decide whether a piece of change should be executed via a project or a programme is another! The following section deals with this decision problem.

Project or programme?

Identifying whether a particular idea for change is a project or programme is an important undertaking, since the right management approach needs to be adopted to ensure the change has a good chance of success. Sometimes it is glaringly obvious, at other times it is more complex. There are no hard and fast rules for every business situation, but some good general guidelines can be compiled. Normally, difficulty will only be encountered with large pieces of change, where the choice is between commissioning a large, complex project or a programme.

Figure 1 shows some examples of business change, categorised as projects or programmes. Those shown as projects could either stand alone or be part of a programme. Local conditions of scope and scale will dictate which of these undertakings are projects or programmes, though size is not the key criterion. A large project could be larger than a programme in terms of resources, cost or scope, but a programme has the characteristics of being complex and multidisciplinary rather

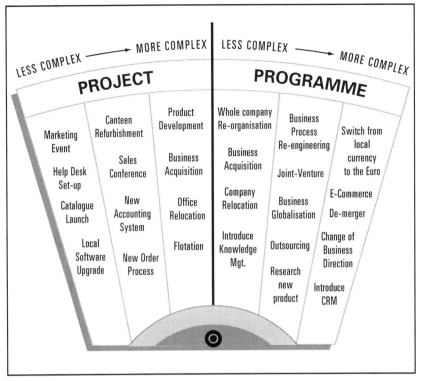

Figure 1 Graduated examples of business projects and programmes

than large in size. The choice for project or programme becomes greyer towards the centre of the fan, and some could equally be both. The problem is that all the projects shown could also be part of a larger programme anyway, so the choice must always be made from asking the question: What is the strategy?

Nearly all of the change featured in Figure 1 relates to business concepts. Some believe that the decision whether to manage change by project or programme is easier for more physical undertakings, such as building a bridge. A bridge is a good example where thinking has to be applied beyond the main construction element. It is unlikely these days that anyone would build a new bridge just for the sake of it. It would usually form part of a strategic requirement. Thus, the bridge would be a major project within a programme that satisfies an objective, say, of communicating between A and B. Other projects within this programme might comprise access infrastructure, environmental replenishment, etc.

The basic reason for a programme is that the proposed change is wide-ranging and strategic. Also, the timescale for the change may be imprecise, particularly if the proposed change is in any way exploratory. A programme can adjust its timescale to suit the outcome of work, changing requirements or changing strategy. It may even become so continuous that it is seen as a fundamental part of a continuing business operation. An example is a support programme, designed to provide support to a community of employees, where projects are commissioned and decommissioned in response to changing requirements from the employees. The programme ends only when the employees no longer require support; but in today's innovatory business environment there is a continuous stream of new products and processes for which the employees need support.

Innovative undertakings, such as research into a new drug, are also well suited to being managed as programmes. At the start there is usually no indication of how the research will turn out, and there is certainly no immediate indication of any end-date.
A good test for identifying whether the desired change is a project or programme is by questioning its scope. The chart opposite shows a simple flow to help you decide on scope grounds.

For example, a plan to roll out several hundred electronic organisers to a company's sales force might well be conceived as a project. The main deliverable focus is the organiser, but there will probably be ancillary deliverables, such as courses for training in organiser use. Question 1 of the model is therefore satisfied. Question 2a does not apply, since, although the roll-out may have several sub-project deliverables, they are not discrete and not related to a wider business strategy. Question 2b is also not satisfied, since the roll-out is not dependent on other change, but will be executed as a single undertaking, even though delivery may be staged over time.

However, in reality, it is unlikely that the roll-out of electronic organisers on any scale would not be part of a strategic initiative. The roll-out is more likely to be one project within a business programme — a programme which satisfies a strategic objective, of, say increasing the efficiency of the sales force. Question two may, therefore, be satisfied, and there may be several discrete projects focusing on the whole concept of sales force efficiency, such as re-appraising the

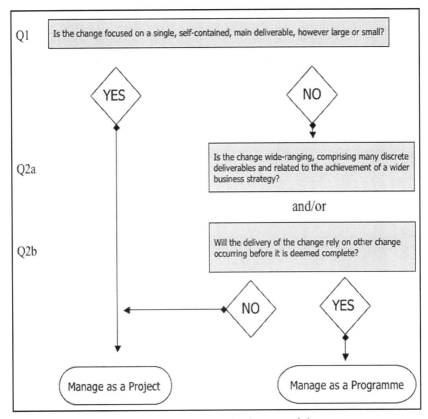

Q1 Is the change focused on a single, self-contained, main deliverable, however large or small?

YES   NO

Q2a Is the change wide-ranging, comprising many discrete deliverables and related to the achievement of a wider business strategy?

and/or

Q2b Will the delivery of the change rely on other change occurring before it is deemed complete?

NO   YES

Manage as a Project   Manage as a Programme

Flow chart for deciding on project or programme by the scope of change

earnings basis of the sales force — something not directly related to the roll-out, but definitely part of the overall efficiency strategy.

The roll-out project has now become part of a wider business plan. Its scope, management and implementation now have the opportunity to be far more assured through its wider association. However, far too few organisations would correctly choose programme management rather than project management as the change vehicle here. The easier option often seems to be to focus on the singular objective as opposed to the larger picture. This action can easily result in duplication of effort, resources and cost, and piecemeal implementations of change.

More enlightened companies have discovered that significant cost savings can be gained by implementing change as strategic programmes. Programme management is, therefore, much in demand as a management approach.

The task of programme identification is becoming a considered undertaking and it is not surprising that OGC devotes a whole stage to programme identification in its programme management framework.

Given the importance of change identification, it is worthwhile establishing a set of questions specific to your company or division for use as a rule of thumb in making sure that desired change is correctly identified as a programme, project or incremental change. I personally feel that, in today's business, no project is truly stand-alone. Perhaps all projects should be thought of as being part of a programme of change. The truly stand-alone project may well be dead.

Summary

Programme management as a structured method is of only recent origin. Its terminology, tools and techniques are still emerging. Its increasing popularity, in spite of its deficiency in tools and techniques, is a reaction to the complexity and wide-ranging nature of today's business change. Certainly, programme management has the ability to tackle complex change over flexible timescales. A key requirement, however, is to be able to differentiate between project and programme. Failure to do this can result in costly duplication of effort and inefficient use of resources.

Companies seeking to embrace programme management as a method should consider how their organisations need to be structured to take full advantage of its benefits. Chapter 2 deals with its applicability to business and its integration into the company structure.

Chapter 2

*a*pplicability to Business

Management of change

Programme management as a structured discipline provides a valuable vehicle for managing strategic change, whether that change be across an entire company or confined to a particular business or departmental function.

Programme management not only allows a business strategy to be broken down into projects and other change vehicles at the outset, but also allows the interpretation of that strategy to be flexible during a programme's lifespan.

The change upon which programmes focus is usually directed from the top of an organisation downwards; it is strategic. A business strategy dictates a change to a business operation and a project or programme is needed to carry it through. It also shows change which is non-strategic (i.e. that which does not require a business strategy, since it does not affect the base purpose of a company's business. This might be, for example, changes to local operating procedures or minor change in response to government regulatory requirements. Non-

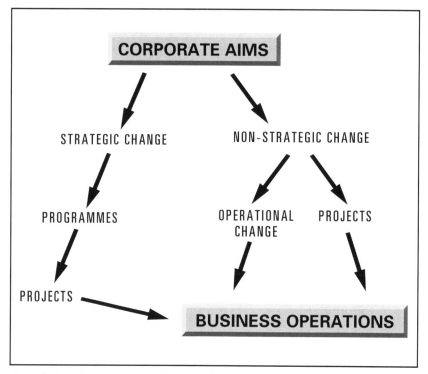

Figure 2 Flow of business change from aims to operation

strategic change can emanate from lower down the organisation and is more likely to do so than strategic change.

At the top of an organisation change typically takes the form of aims or ideas, with direction being given to functional heads to execute that change in whichever way they feel empowered. This is not normally a problem for non-strategic change, but could cause difficulties where the change is strategic. Conveying strategic change in this way is open to misinterpretation by individual functions and also devolves executive control.

Whole-company strategic change is particularly vulnerable. Some hard lessons have been learned through the implementation of changes required to deliver e-commerce, for example, where executive direction to individual divisions has been at the idea level, instead of at an organised programme level. This has resulted in differing interpretations of the change requirements by each division. It may have been convenient for corporations to direct divisions to establish

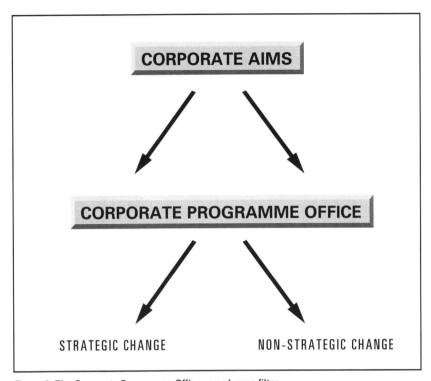

Figure 3 The Corporate Programme Office as a change filter

an e-commerce plan and report back progress, but without guidance from the centre such a direction is foolhardy. Ultimately, if things go wrong in any one division, shareholders will blame the corporation, not the division.

Increasingly, strategic change is being mapped and planned at the top of the organisation, and *corporate programme offices* are being constructed to filter corporate aims and ideas into the correct change channels. These are permanent offices that commission and track company change as programmes and projects, rolling up progress from individual managers and reporting it to the board. The concept is not new. I first assisted with the implementation of such an office at the headquarters of a UK retail finance organisation in 1988. Over 60 projects or programmes were regularly on the "books" at any one time, ranging from the refurbishment of the front of the building (a Premises Department project) to the implementation of computing technology in support of high-street outlets (an IT Department programme). The corporate programme office, or corporate change office, as it might be more appropriately called, ensured that each project or programme was properly represented in terms of sponsorship, funding, resources and corporate priority.

In today's business environment, where whole-company change occurs with increasing regularity, such a corporate structure provides considerable benefits. It ensures that programmes and projects are given the right business priority and that they get off to a good start. Programme management, therefore, sits more comfortably within this sort of corporate structure.

An example of whole-company change in the 1990s was the Inland Revenue's *Self Assessment Programme.* One of the largest programmes ever undertaken by the public sector, it directly affected nine million taxpayers, 85,000 agents, 350,000 employers and 25,000 Revenue employees. By any standards this was a huge undertaking. It involved the design and construction of one of the world's largest computer systems (through a partnership with EDS), together with the introduction of complex legislation in three Finance Acts. The programme had to be undertaken against an implementation date which had been fixed by legislative statute, and against a background of uncertain political support: a change in UK government in May, 1997 caused particular anxiety.

A review team highlighted certain key factors which contributed to the overall success of this programme, among which was the use of a "dedicated programme office to provide a single source of reliable information and a variety of support services". Another was "making Self Assessment the Department's number one priority and living that commitment in decisions and actions". Chapter 6 shows that commitment to purpose is a key success criterion for programmes and that faith in the outcome can make or break a programme.

The Inland Revenue success story demonstrates that management of change is much more than the employment of a structured method. It requires real partnership (both internally and with third parties) and a commitment and determination to succeed from the top of the organisation downwards.

Duration of programmes and change components

Projects are transient in nature. They tend to come and go, but ought to have defined start and end dates. However, projects which are of long duration, in excess, say, of nine months, run a greater risk of scope change, as a result of changing business requirements and market conditions.

Business programmes tend to be of longer duration than projects. One would expect to see programmes lasting in excess of nine months duration. Two-year programmes are not uncommon, and I have witnessed longer programmes lasting four or even ten years. Their end-dates tend to be less fixed than projects and, like lengthy projects, they are also subject to scope change. However, programmes should be designed for scope change since their very longevity makes changes almost certain. A two-year information technology programme, for example, is unlikely to implement exactly the same technology as conceived at its outset. Technology and the marketplace moves on.

Thus, a critical difference between programme and project management is the handling of changes. Programme management should allow for change as a normal occurrence, rather than as an exceptional occurrence, as is the case with projects.

It is conceivable that the viability of a complete programme could be questioned if changes in technology or the marketplace are particularly pronounced. For example, the British Library programme suffered a period of soul searching when it was thought that the original justification for the work might be less valid in future years. Planned in 1978 for an opening date in the late 1980s, the programme was conceived as providing a new, purpose-built building to house the national collection of books and provide storage for future acquisitions. The original 1850s building in Bloomsbury, London, was running out of space. There were ancillary benefits, but the main requirement was for more space, planned against an assumption that the bound book would be around for many years to come.

During the 1980s the development of the electronic book challenged this preconception. There was a very real possibility that at some not-too-distant future date, books, in the format that we know them, might generally cease to exist. With electronic books, of course, shelf space becomes redundant. Newspaper reports in July, 1994, started to question the whole programme's viability, particularly as it was reported to be heavily over-budget, over-running, "burgeoning out of control" and unlikely to provide space even for the existing collections. Even the architecture of the new building in St. Pancras was described by one newspaper as "one of the ugliest buildings in the world".

A rethink of the programme was necessary. It was to the credit of Sir Anthony Kenny, who became Chairman of the British Library Board in 1993, that the programme was turned round to face a realistic scope change. Construction was completed in early 1997 and new public services planned. The building was finally opened to the public on 24 November, 1997.

The bound book will probably exist for many years, but, very quickly, electronic versions will almost certainly become the norm. Most authors now produce their manuscripts in electronic format (as is the case with this book) and send them to publishers on disk or via electronic mail. The British Library has already embarked on a programme of conversion of important books and manuscripts to electronic formats using image technology, which, being available for consultation via email, may avoid the need for a reader to visit the library in person. Rare manuscripts can be saved from excessive physical handling and the readership can be extended to a worldwide audience via the Internet. Thus, the lack of storage space and reader seats bemoaned in 1994 will be solved by the march of technology.

Programme management did not help the British Library initially, since it was not conceived as a unified programme, but as a series of related projects. Few companies could say in 1978 that they recognised programme management as a management discipline. As I pointed out earlier in the introduction, programme management has really come of age through the need to embark on whole-company change, such as Year 2000, European Monetary Union and company re-engineering.

Figure 4 shows the typical project constituents of a programme for a business transitioning from traditional trading to e-commerce. Such programmes reflect the need to effect radical changes to a business in order to take advantage of the trading benefits afforded by technology.

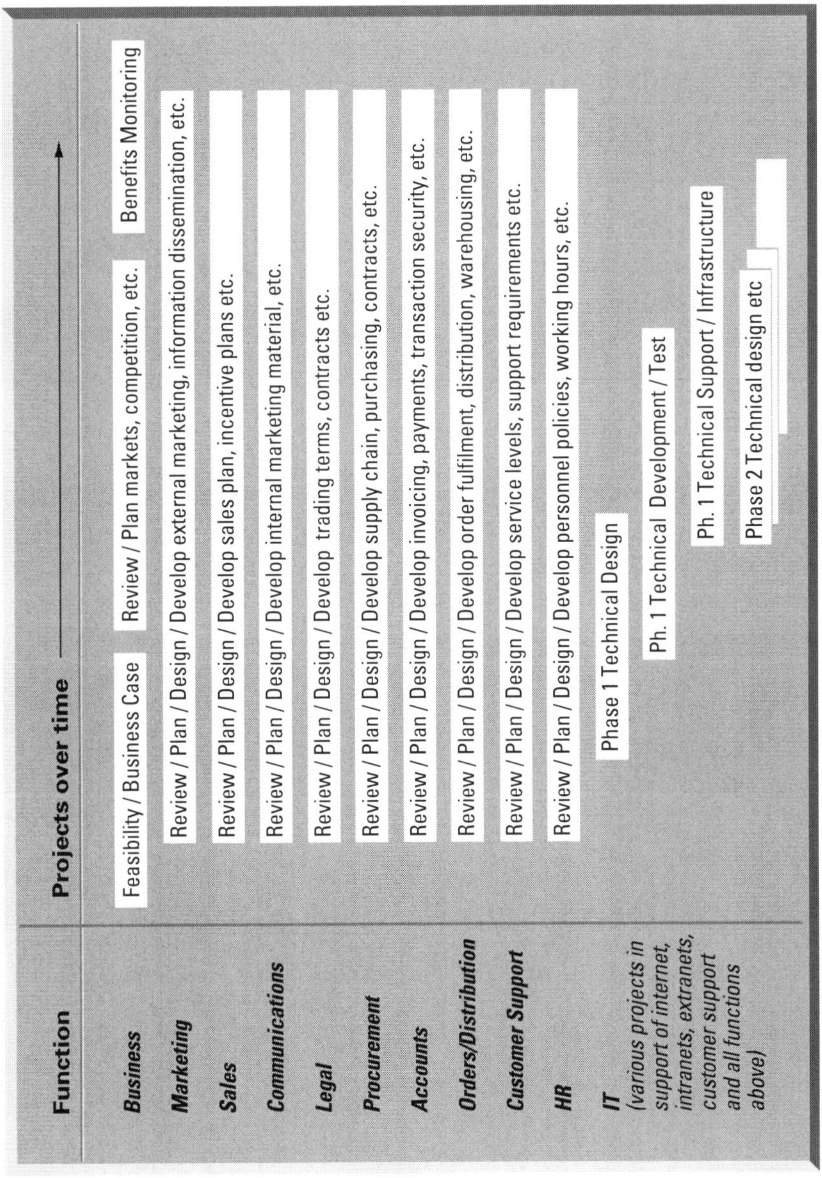

Figure 4 Schematic of a typical transition to e-commerce programme

Function	Projects over time		
	Feasibility / Business Case	Review / Plan markets, competition, etc.	Benefits Monitoring
Business			
Marketing		Review / Plan / Design / Develop external marketing, information dissemination, etc.	
Sales		Review / Plan / Design / Develop sales plan, incentive plans etc.	
Communications		Review / Plan / Design / Develop internal marketing material, etc.	
Legal		Review / Plan / Design / Develop trading terms, contracts etc.	
Procurement		Review / Plan / Design / Develop supply chain, purchasing, contracts, etc.	
Accounts		Review / Plan / Design / Develop invoicing, payments, transaction security, etc.	
Orders/Distribution		Review / Plan / Design / Develop order fulfilment, distribution, warehousing, etc.	
Customer Support		Review / Plan / Design / Develop service levels, support requirements etc.	
HR		Review / Plan / Design / Develop personnel policies, working hours, etc.	
IT *(various projects in support of internet, intranets, extranets, customer support and all functions above)*	Phase 1 Technical Design	Ph. 1 Technical Development / Test	
		Ph. 1 Technical Support / Infrastructure	
		Phase 2 Technical design etc	

However, as they progress, the concept of e-commerce becomes less defined, making it part of the fabric, so to speak. Such programmes tend to roll on, taking advantage of new developments in technology and reacting to competitive pressures. A decision has to be taken at some point to say that the desired change of state has taken place and the programme has achieved its benefits.

It is not unusual for programmes to include whole-programme decision checkpoints. Some programme management methods mandate these, and extend them to breathing spaces of weeks or even months. There is only so much change an organisation can take in one go, and it is useful to be able to stand back and take stock of what has been accomplished, and to take advantage of the benefits delivered so far.

Implementing a corporate programme office

Today's companies have to react with increasing frequency to external changes. Many of these changes radically alter the way products are manufactured or sold or the way services are offered. Such radical change requires a company to react in order to compete. The ability of a company to react often depends on how good is its decision-making. The quality of its decision-making depends partly on the quality of its decision-makers and partly on the completeness of its data. This latter is especially important, since no matter how good are the decision-makers, if the data is incomplete or of poor quality then the decisions will be flawed.

The Corporate Programme Office is designed to enable companies to react quickly to radical change. It does this by monitoring the execution of change to ensure that benefits are achieved in line with business and financial expectations and by treating change as a corporate asset. There are still too many companies managing change in organisational silos, which results in increased costs, duplication of effort and inefficient distribution of benefits.

The logical implementation of strategic blueprints is via programmes and projects; but these need to be locked into a controlling function at corporate level. Such a function is the Corporate Programme Office, which seeks to derive value from the change programmes it controls. Establishing such a function brings considerable benefits to a company, not least through knowing the committed level of change being undertaken at any one time, its risk exposure, priority, cost and benefits. Implementation of the function, however, requires an organisational and mindset change that some long-in-the-tooth companies could find difficult to embrace.

It only needs one major market change, however, to focus the mind. A good example of this was the sudden introduction of direct insurance selling to the UK market in 1994, through an initiative by the Royal Bank of Scotland. At a stroke, this challenged the time-honoured practice of using intermediaries to sell insurance. Boosted by information technology providing better and faster data, the risks of selling insurance directly were mitigated. The insurance industry was caught unawares. Not only had someone made it possible to sell insurance directly, but the initiative had not even come from within the insurance industry, but from a bank!

To make matters worse, it was also very successful. So much so, that insurance companies vied to implement their own direct channels as fast as possible. This proved problematic, however, for several reasons. To launch a direct channel quickly needed ready cash, and many had already spent their budgets for the year on other initiatives. The alternative was to review existing business programmes and see what could be axed. However, many failed to understand the exact nature, cost and progress of their current change initiatives, simply because corporate control of change was inadequate. I was consulting to a UK insurance company at the time and remember the hasty scrabble to get data on existing programmes within each department. How many days do you think it should have taken? Three at the most? Guess six weeks and you would be nearer the mark. Taking several weeks to establish a current set of figures is hardly an ability to react to a fast-moving marketplace. Ironically, the reason for my consultancy was to discuss with the Board the establishment of a Corporate Programme Office! With such a function the data should have been immediately available to a certain currency, sufficient at least for the Board to make initial decisions.

For the insurance industry, with the launch of a direct channel, the market had changed overnight. It would not have been possible without the availability of better information, assisted by information technology.

IT has since engendered further radical market changes, making the need for the Corporate Programme Office function even more urgent.

A later example is, of course, the Year 2000 computing problem. Even before the problem could be assessed company-wide, accurate inventories needed to be established. The time taken to establish these inventories varied enormously, depending on the state of records and configuration management practices. A sound lesson to be learned from Year 2000 is that the retention and accessibility of corporate knowledge are of vital importance for today's business. If anyone doubts it may ever be used again to the extent that Year 2000 demanded, then think only of the company-wide implications of European monetary union and e-commerce. Again, those companies which can absorb this major change and remain competitive will thrive.

Figure 6 in Chapter 3 shows how the Corporate Programme Office can control an entire company change structure. Every piece of change is linked back from project to change strategy.

Cost of programmes

Programmes are not portfolios of projects bundled together for the sake of convenience. A programme has its own management and administrative infrastructure. It is, therefore, a costly undertaking.

The true cost of a programme comprises the cost of resources, materials, premises and equipment plus its risk exposure (see Chapter 6), and is only apparent once a certain stage of a programme has been reached. The cost becomes clearer as each stage is progressed, so estimates have to be agreed for each stage:

Stage	Cost approach
Business Strategy	Rough estimate for budgetary purposes
Change Blueprint	Rough estimate for change vehicles plus risk element
Programme Feasibility / Business Case	Feasibility estimates plus risk exposure for management approval
Programme Design	More assured estimates for each change vehicle plus overall risk exposure

These stages are convenient sign-off points for budgetary purposes as well as feasibility. The thoroughness of the estimates and the approvals required will depend on existing company approval processes. Some companies will want to go out to tender for a whole programme or various parts of a programme. The earliest feasible point for inviting tenders is during the latter phases of Programme Feasibility. Final contracts, however, need the detail of a Programme Design to be of real value and some companies would prefer to wait until this stage before inviting tenders. Many potential suppliers, however, would prefer to be involved in the detail of Programme Design than be offered a fait accompli. A more assured contract can be constructed if suppliers are able to be party to the design process.

Against the cost of a programme must be weighed its benefits. Each project and change vehicle will contribute, but some projects may only be cost effective when considered as part of a programme. Considered individually they may not be cost effective. Benefits need to be quantified from the outset, but like costs, only rough estimates can probably be given at first. For each benefit a measurement vehicle needs to be decided, together with its source. For example, a benefit of saving telephone calls for the introduction of a local number operation might be stated as:

Benefit
Reduction in cost of telephone calls

Measurement vehicle
Number and cost of non-local calls against local calls

Measurement source
Telephone service invoice breakdown

(See Chapter 7 for more information on benefits management throughout a programme's lifespan.)

I find it difficult to conceive setting a budget for an entire programme at its outset. The longer a programme is in duration, the more uncertain the outcome. For a programme to remain flexible in its execution of a business strategy, it needs to be unhindered as much as possible by time and cost. Financial managers tend not to like too much flexibility in cost, preferring to earmark a budget for the duration. Experience, however, shows that setting budgets by stage is preferable to an overall budget. The London 2012 Olympics Programme, for example, has suffered somewhat through its fixed end-date for the hosting of the Olympic Games and many perceiving it to be a single deliverable, and so suited to having a fixed overall budget. This is very much "large project" speak and not at all in keeping with the concept of "programme". The strategy behind the programme includes land regeneration, so the programme will continue for some time after the games have been held. Building an Olympic Park is a series of projects within a much wider programme. Those criticising the programme for its inevitable budget increases need to understand this scope.

Implementing a programme management method

The real benefit to be obtained from programme management is the adoption of a common company approach to the management of programmes. Many companies have adopted particular approaches and tools for project management and can do the same for programme management. Of course, implementing a programme management method presupposes that a project management method will be implemented or already exists.

Unfortunately, programme management methods have yet to reach the same sort of maturity as project management methods. Fully comprehensive methods are few and far between, but some companies have managed to create their own approaches, either working from scratch or adapting others. Some have taken OGC's open approach and written low-level guidance for users, while others have taken a more tools-oriented direction. Few software programs, though, have been constructed specifically for programme management. Many software applications designed for project management claim to cater for programme management. However, tools are not a substitute for a good method.

The successful implementation of a programme management method must be set against a current company culture for embracing change and the use of structured methods. It will not be easy in some organisations. Household Finance Bank, for example, was able to establish a structure to co-ordinate all of its UK change initiatives, whereby all change is linked firmly to business strategy and co-ordinated centrally under a Director of Corporate Co-ordination. The structure has been stable for more than twenty years, so it is clearly embedded in the company culture.

Implementing programme management within the context of corporate change management brings significant efficiency and cost savings. Increasingly, companies are being forced to address their whole approach to change management, since whole-company change is becoming a fact of life. The re-engineering of a corporation may need to take place several times during forthcoming decades, either as a reaction to competition and the marketplace or through acquisitions, mergers, de-mergers, downsizing and the outsourcing of functional activities.

Summary

Programmes deliver strategic change, and are best managed in an environment which recognises the importance of change management. Today's penchant for whole-company change is well served by programme management. Having a Corporate Programme Office as part of a company structure is a particular benefit in the translation of strategic ideas to practical change, and enables programmes and projects to be properly prioritised and positioned. It also enables companies to react quickly to changes in the marketplace.

Programmes are costly ventures, but the benefits they bring usually justify their undertaking. Companies should only embark on programmes if they accept that change during the life of a programme is inevitable. Few programmes are of short enough duration to escape a change in composition or scope. Today's rapidly changing marketplace gives testimony to that.

Chapter 3

*M*oving from Business Strategy to Programme Design

This chapter deals with the difficult task of translating strategic change into a viable programme. It is the closest this book comes to methodology, but I believe that a structured guide through the critical stages is more value to the reader than commentary. These stages reflect my own experience.

Moving from a strategy for change to a fully planned delivery programme may feel like a leap in the dark. It requires a translation of what is often blue-sky thinking to a feasible, quantified scope. There are always revelations and in some cases the strategy is just not feasible. I remember a principal of a university once showed me a beautifully produced, glossy booklet which set out a vision of change for the next five years. Apart from the dates the booklet did not contain any numbers. It had been produced at not inconsiderable expense by a firm of management consultants. The principal had a clear requirement in mind, though: "What I want you to do, John, is to turn this into a delivery programme"! Unfortunately, an unrealistic expectation of cost and the number of resources required meant that

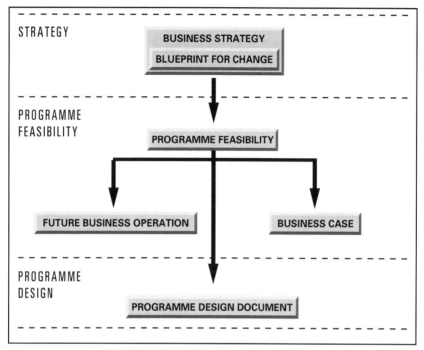

Figure 5 The three stages of programme inception

the strategy could not be translated in its current form. However, it highlights how important it is to consider the translation from strategy to delivery in a number of defined stages, each of which should have a go/no-go stage-gate decision.

Figure 2 in Chapter 2 shows the flow of business change from corporate aims to operation. Programmes are born out of strategic change but, before they can be conceived, a Business Strategy needs to be constructed that outlines the scope of the strategic change. There are three main stages involved in the birth of a programme:

1. Business Strategy

2. Programme Feasibility

3. Programme Design

Most programme management methodologies agree on these basic components, but the terminology and number of stages may be different.

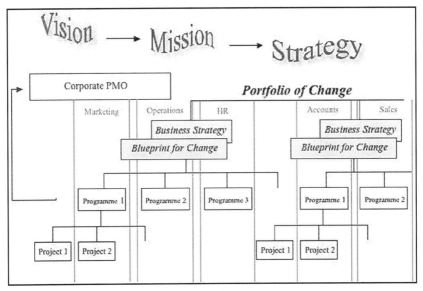

Figure 6   Schematic of a portfolio of company change

Figure 5 shows the logical progression from Business Strategy to Programme Design via Programme Feasibility.

Business Strategy to Change Blueprint

It is beyond the scope of this book to specify the contents of a Business Strategy, since each company will have its own way of producing such a document. However, in this context a Business Strategy should outline the aims and desired directions of a business and will probably specify goals, objectives, risks, an outline of the current business operation, and the reasons for business change.

It is good practice to keep a Business Strategy document as a high-level series of business goals, specifying the change objectives that will meet those goals in a separate, but related document. This separate document may be referred to as the Blueprint for Change, since it effectively becomes the mode for implementing the Business Strategy. A reason for keeping the two documents separate is that it is likely that the Blueprint will change more than the Strategy itself, and there is no point in updating two documents regularly. Figure 6 shows a representation of a corporate portfolio of change, comprising several business strategies. These are shown in the

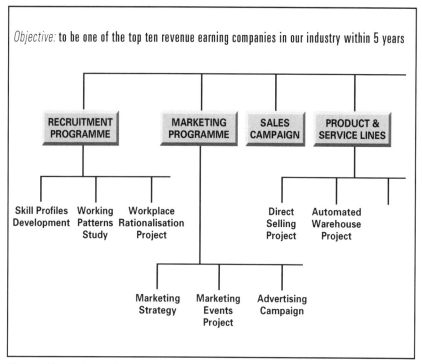

Figure 7 Extract from a Change Blueprint schematic showing change vehicles

context of various company functions (Marketing, Operations, etc.).

The Blueprint might identify one or more programmes as well as standalone projects and local operational initiatives, depending on the scale and scope of the desired change. For example, in the Annual Report of XYZ Machine Tools, the Chairman might announce a strategy for improving service to customers. The strategy states several goals related to improving service. Sufficient vehicles need to be identified to execute the strategy and achieve the desired change. Senior management interpret the strategy and produce a document entitled Blueprint for Valued Customers. The Blueprint identifies a programme to improve customer satisfaction, with suggested projects in each of seven departments, plus a separate programme to change the way products are sold. Both initiatives are necessary to achieve the goals of the strategy, but may be executed as separate vehicles of change.

In another example, a company wishes to execute a strategy to become one of the top ten companies in its industry sector. Figure 7 shows an

Contents	Interpretation or origin
Strategic goals	Summary of goals from the Business Strategy
Change objectives	Objectives which will meet the Business Strategy goals
Change feasibility	An indication of what can be achieved over what time period
Change benefits	Summary of perceived benefits from the Business Strategy
Outline future business operation	A sketch of the company or business function after implementation of the Blueprint
Vehicles for change	A list of potential programmes, projects and local initiatives, and their priorities for implementation
Outline costs	A rough first estimate of the costs of implementing the Blueprint, (e.g. human resources, equipment, facilities, marketing, support and maintenance)
Risk assessment	An assessment of the risks of implementing the Blueprint

Table 2 Typical contents of a Blueprint for Change

extract from a Blueprint of the sort of programmes, projects and change vehicles that might be necessary.

There is no template for a Change Blueprint, since companies will want to write such a document according to their own style. It should, however, include a risk assessment for embarking on the desired change plus the usual business and financial assessments for this type of document. Besides suggesting vehicles for change, the Blueprint should also specify some aspects of future business operation and the feasibility of the overall Strategy.

Table 2 summarises the typical contents of a Change Blueprint. Although the Blueprint can stand alone as a single document it is important to ensure that it maintains strong links with the Business Strategy and the feasibility studies it will spawn. Note that the Blueprint specifies the objectives for the Business Strategy's goals. It does not have its own goals.

IBM UK Ltd. produced a classic Blueprint in 1990, when, under the leadership of Nick Temple, the company underwent a massive cultural re-organisation in preparation for changing the company from a purely hardware manufacturer and supplier to a fifty per cent software and services company. The document was known simply as *Blueprint for the Nineties* and spawned several programmes, initiatives and projects in support of the overall strategy.

The Blueprint should have an owner, since it needs to be updated in line with change implementation progress, organisational and operational changes and any changes to the Business Strategy. Some organisations nominate the same owner for the Blueprint as the Business Strategy, but it may be another individual; ideally, someone who will champion the Blueprint's contents.

Programme Feasibility

The next step in the change process is to establish separately the feasibility of each change vehicle mentioned in the Blueprint. This can be a significant undertaking and is likely to be the first significant cost expenditure of the process, so it should only be embarked upon once there is general agreement that the Blueprint is sound. This affirmation should mean that the Business Strategy is also sound, and that the goals of the Strategy are sufficiently covered by the objectives of the Blueprint in order to make it achievable.

Programme Feasibility is the first stage in the lifespan of an individual programme, but for many programmes it is also the last. Many never reach the consequent *Programme Design* stage, since their viability is not confirmed. However, the money spent in assessing a programme's feasibility is rarely wasted, since knowledge will be acquired for useful future use. It is better to reject a programme at this stage than discover its inappropriateness later and at greater cost. Feasibility is often a circular event, with the Blueprint being revisited in order to make adjustments to the scope of change.

During the Feasibility stage, a *Business Case* will need to be prepared, which will confirm the viability of the programme in terms of costs, resources and benefits. Table 3 shows the typical contents. It is also useful to construct a map of the *future business operation* that the

Contents	Interpretation or origin
Programme goals	*Goals which support the Change Blueprint objectives*
Programme objectives	*Objectives which will meet the programme goals*
Programme feasibility	*Reason for the programme and its feasibility, timescale etc.*
Programme benefits	*Quantified benefits from the programme, which support the benefits from the Change Blueprint*
Outline future business operation	*A sketch of the company or business function after implementation of the programme*
Outline resource plan	*Estimate of resources required for the life of the programme*
Outline costs	*Estimate of the costs of implementing the programme, (e.g. human resources, equipment, facilities, marketing, support and maintenance), together with risk exposure cost (Ch.7)*
Risk assessment	*An assessment of the risks of implementing the programme*

Table 3 Typical contents of a Business Case

programme will bring about. This will be linked to the similar, but higher level, future business outline in the Blueprint. The document at the programme level will be a useful yardstick for the role of Business Change Manager (see Chapter 5) in monitoring the expected benefits of the programme. It is, therefore, desirable for the Business Change Manager to be appointed at Programme Feasibility stage in order to help draw up the Business Case.

Programme Feasibility is completed once sufficient information has been gathered to enable a decision to be made concerning the viability of the programme. It is not worth compiling too much detail of the programme's design during the Feasibility stage in case approval to move to the Design stage is not forthcoming. However, enough needs to be known in order to compile a reasonable Business Case. The Programme Design stage will, of course, produce much more detail, and the Business Case can then be enhanced.

It is important not to launch into Programme Design too quickly, since it too can be a costly exercise. Many companies employ external consultants to assist with the production of Change Blueprints and feasibility studies. Their impartiality is often a key requirement for tackling what are often sensitive areas of business change. However, few companies are so well organised that descriptions of business processes and operations are readily to hand and are up to date. Usually, there is significant research needed in order to gather the necessary data, and it is unlikely that production of a Change Blueprint, for example, could be accomplished in less than six weeks for a medium-size programme.

Designing a programme

Once the feasibility of a programme has been agreed, the programme can proceed to the design stage known as *Programme Design*. During this stage a design document is constructed that sets out the scope and structure of the programme. It is initially a high-level view, since it will not be known at the outset exactly how many projects will be commissioned during the life of the programme. It is continually reviewed, and will become a basis for steering the programme and evaluating any changes of direction. Some refer to this document as the Programme Blueprint, but throughout this book it will be referred to as the Programme Design Document in order to avoid any confusion with the Change Blueprint.

What needs to be designed? There are several key elements of design that need to be considered, and certain minimal decisions need to be taken in order to ensure that the programme gets off to a good start. These are:

1. **The business reason for the programme**
a brief statement from the Change Blueprint of the business benefits of the programme

2. **Goals and objectives of the programme**
those which support the goals and objectives of the Blueprint and Business Strategy

3. **Programme scope, boundaries and assumptions**
what the programme does and does not encompass, its constraints, external dependencies and assumptions

Business Strategy Goal 1 (Euro): Maintain the ability to trade during the changeover to the Euro without degradation of service or quality. *Other goals*
Change Blueprint Objective 1 (Euro) : Achieve Euro readiness across all divisions of the company by the end of 2001. *Other objectives*
Corporate Euro Programme Goal 1 : Ensure all IT systems are Euro compliant Goal 2 : Ensure all business processes are Euro compliant Goal 3 : Ensure key suppliers interfacing with the company are Euro compliant. Goal 4 : Ensure customers are aware of changes being made. Goal 5 : Ensure no degradation or loss of service to customers. Goal 6 : Ensure sufficient training is provided to retail staff. *Other goals* *Other objectives*
IT Project Goal 1 : Ensure critical business programs are Euro compliant Goal 2 : Ensure continuity of service during code conversion and testing Goal 3 : Ensure disaster recovery procedures are up to date *Other goals* *Other objectives*

Table 4 Example of hierarchy of goals and objectives from Business Strategy to Project

4. Work elements and priorities
what work the programme needs to undertake and its perceived projects

5. Timescale
the phasing of the programme into manageable pieces of work

6. Organisation and roles
the programme's organisation structure, roles and responsibilities

7. Programme support
the management method, tracking and measurement, and administrative structure (Programme Office)

8. Risks and issues

the main risks and issues currently known, collected from items 1-7 above.

The above are shown in the order in which they are usually designed. If Programme Feasibility has been done well then Programme Design is merely taking feasibility to the next level of detail. There should be no fundamental questions during Programme Design regarding the Business Strategy or programme viability. If there are, it is unwise to proceed to Design.

Programme goals and objectives

The programme goals and objectives must support those of the Blueprint and Business Strategy. The Change Blueprint is effectively the implementation plan for the Business Strategy and has objectives that underwrite the goals of the Business Strategy. Thus the pathway from Business Strategy to programme is: *Business Strategy goals* to *Change Blueprint objectives* to *programme goals and objectives.*

From the Blueprint it will be clear which segment of the overall change the programme is designed to undertake, so there should be a good starting point for defining the programme's goals. In defining programme goals and objectives it should not be forgotten that the goals and objectives for individual projects will need to fit below those of the programme. Thus a hierarchy of goals and objectives is established from Business Strategy to individual project, as shown in the example in Table 4. Standard business techniques may be used for their definition.

Objectives should be clear and unambiguous and, where possible, should be quantifiable. Many people find the task of defining objectives to be difficult because of this, but if a programme is to be clear in its execution and delivery there should be no doubt about the clarity of the objectives. The main rule is to ensure that there are sufficient objectives to cover the aim of each goal. Thus Goal 4 of the Corporate Euro Programme in Table 4 should have objectives which cover services, customers, quality and products. Some goals may need only a single objective, whilst others may need multiple objectives.

Scope, boundaries and assumptions

The programme scope states what the programme does and does not encompass. It may be expressed in terms of geography, markets, divisions of the company and departments affected, products, services, processes, systems, personnel, suppliers and customers. Dependencies on other programmes, projects or company initiatives should also be considered and mapped.

The scope is often a choice of what is feasible and what is desirable, and, since the latter may not be feasible currently but might well be in the future, it is useful to document both views for later reference. The scope should also state any constraints placed upon it in terms of resources, timescale, budget, etc.

The scope should relate to the programme goals and objectives and be quite clear in its content. A scope which is not explicit could cause problems for the programme later.

The scope should also include key assumptions regarding the programme. For example:

- *it is assumed that the Northern District warehouse will not be relocated before programme completion*

- *it is assumed that Transport Division will provide office space and facilities for the XYZ Project*

- *it is assumed that the Programme Office will be sited at Head Office*

Assumptions need to be ratified before the programme gets under way. This is in order to avoid having to make costly changes to the programme at a later date when particular assumptions are found to be invalid. Also, assumptions often imply risk, so may need to be added as risks to the risk register.

Constructing the scope may be accomplished using similar processes for the construction of a project scope. A good initial approach is to organise a workshop for key decision-makers. Several iterations may be necessary before the scope is deemed sound.

Work elements and priorities
This part of the Design states the types of work that need to be undertaken in order to identify the programme's constituent projects.

Each piece of work must relate to the programme goals and objectives and be within its scope. The work is prioritised and apportioned into projects, each of which needs to be scoped and defined at a later date.

Projects will have been suggested in the Change Blueprint, according to work elements known at the time. During Programme Design, these projects are ratified or amended. Any significant changes are fed back to the Blueprint. It is unlikely that the work elements will change from Blueprint to programme scope, but their organisation into projects might.

For example, programme work elements such as *establish a customer support centre* and *devise customer support policy* could be grouped into a project called *Customer Support*. How much can be accomplished in terms of work breakdown for individual projects at this stage depends on the expertise of the programme designers. It is not necessary to go to a fine level of detail, since this will be done later by those having a greater knowledge of the project. However, a starter set of work elements would be useful when each project embarks on its scoping, e.g.

Customer Care Project
Produce project plan
  Establish a customer support centre
    Establish terms of reference
    Draw up space requirements
      Select location
    Assess facilities and equipment
      Place equipment orders
      Lay cables
    Staff centre
      Produce job descriptions
      Recruit staff
      Train staff
  Devise customer support policy
      Produce training manuals
      Publicise service

It may only be possible to construct a rough work breakdown structure for each project. Often there will be precedents for repeatable work such as the establishment of a customer support centre, and

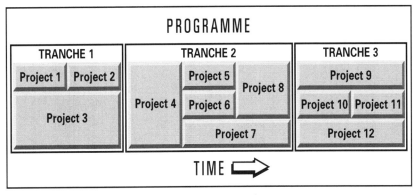

Table 5 A programme and its projects divided into tranches

template work breakdown structures may exist within the company, upon which designers can draw. A repository of previous project experience is also useful for the scoping exercise, although few companies have such a luxury available. Having a work breakdown structure facilitates the assignment of responsibilities and the project's organisation into sub-projects.

Timescale

Only an outline of the programme timescale can be given at Design stage, as individual projects will not have been scoped and planned. Certain time related considerations should be examined here, however, such as the effects of the implementation of major change on the workforce. Should, for example, the programme be broken down into blocks of work with periods of normal business operation in between? Many refer to these blocks as *tranches* (from the French word for "slice"), which are themselves almost mini-programmes. It is sometimes preferable to divide programmes of several years in length into time or work based tranches. Table 5 shows this idea.

Unlike a project, a programme may not have a defined end-date at its outset. It is often not appropriate. The programme completes either when the last piece of strategic change from its objectives is implemented or the business benefits are declared achieved. Many programmes change their shape and direction several times before "time is called". It is this flexibility of timescale that enables programmes to be such useful vehicles for change.

Organisation and roles

Deciding on the programme roles and completing the organisation chart is a fundamental part of Programme Design. Chapter 4 covers this important work in detail.

Programme support

A programme, like a project, requires an administrative infrastructure to support its day-to-day activities. The centre of this activity is within the Programme Office (which is described in detail in Chapter 6).

A programme also requires a management method, which will specify what will be managed, by whom and how. The method should state, for example, how benefits and quality will be managed; and a good method will include structures and techniques for these and for other functions. Typical management functions include:

- quality (including deliverables and testing)
- benefits
- design
- programme exceptions (risks, issues, changes)
- costs, expenses, payments, budget
- personnel time, performance
- time schedule, milestones, dependencies
- contracts
- documentation
- health and safety.

Risks and issues

Several risks and maybe some issues will have been identified during Programme Feasibility. These should be carried forward into Programme Design. The process of risk management should already have started and it is helpful to have a Risk Manager appointed as early as possible during the programme's lifespan. Construction of a Risk Register will be helpful at this stage. This can be passed to the Programme Office, when it is established.

The management of programme risk is discussed in detail in Chapter 7.

Summary

Designing business programmes is a professional task, and best undertaken by experienced programme management consultants. The most difficult aspect is the transition from Business Strategy to Programme Design. Considerable ground work needs to be accomplished and there is often a temptation to move forward too quickly in the vital preparatory stages. Use of the structured approach described, however, should ensure that key aspects are not missed, that expectations are adequately established and that there is confidence in the outcome.

Chapter 4

*O*rganising a Programme

During the Programme Feasibility stage some thought will have been given to key programme roles. These should be confirmed during the Programme Design stage, where the remaining roles and the structure in which they reside are established. Programmes have been known to succeed or fail merely on the choice of leaders and the designation of their authority. Because a programme is close to the heart of a business it becomes part of the company fabric, so it must not be left unattended; sadly the case of many business projects. The programme must also be accorded the correct level of priority within the company.

There is general agreement in programme methodologies that a *Programme Manager* must be appointed. This is the person accountable for the day-to-day management of the programme. It should normally be a full-time role, but could be part-time, depending upon the size, scope and activity of the programme. A relatively inactive programme (ie, with few currently commissioned projects) could justify a part-time Programme Manager. Aspects of this role are described later in this Chapter.

The roles described in this chapter are those which I have utilised successfully. People often ask me whether it is necessary to implement all of the roles described. The answer must be that any change, which requires a programme to undertake it, is going to be costly; stinting on resources is bound to have an effect on its quality. The key decision criteria are to ensure that a bureaucratic organisation is not established, that roles are filled sufficient to the requirement at a particular stage, and that there is also flexibility to adjust roles throughout a programme's life.

It is, therefore, essential to plan the resource requirement during the Design stage with reference to the planned complement of projects. If, for example, the programme is planned to commence with only one project, which is only a preparatory piece of work, then there is no point in immediately establishing a full programme staff. Figure 4 shows a complement of several projects and initiatives which kick off in parallel, and are augmented at the end of the first year. It would be inappropriate here to commence with a skeleton staff. Also, the phases shown represent very different types and intensity of work. This needs to be taken into account when assessing the organisation requirements for this type of programme.

It is easy to be dismissive about programme management, treating it as being just a larger piece of work than project management, but the skills are very different. A programme that is not tightly controlled will overrun on costs and deliver reduced benefits. The risks of not being in control are higher when programme roles are not recognised as requiring professional skills – not any person from a business function can be a Programme Manager, for example.

Major programmes can benefit from employing an experienced programme consultant to assist in building an appropriate organisation structure and selecting the right candidates for particular roles. Indeed, many companies value consultancy advice for the whole of the crucial Design stage.

The Programme Executive

In my experience, the Programme Manager is not an isolated role, unlike that of a Project Manager. To be effective, the programme needs

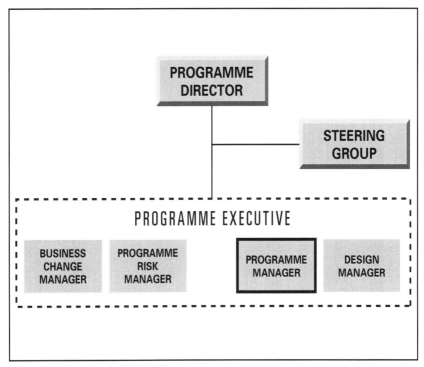

Figure 8 A typical Programme Executive

to be managed by an executive team. The Programme Manager is still accountable, and designated *leader*, but is supported by a management team, which makes up the core team or *Programme Executive*. These are senior roles and represent the business and technical aspects of the programme.

The reason for having a management team instead of a single manager is that managing a programme is similar to managing a business. A business in the private sector would have an executive team and in the public sector there may be a similar high-level team providing leadership. The London Olympics 2012 Programme, for example, has a Programme Executive entitled the Olympic Delivery Authority (ODA).

The numbers and types of roles within the Programme Executive will vary according to the need of the programme and the programme method employed. Figure 8 shows a typical generic set, where the Programme Manager is supported by a Business Change Manager, Risk Manager and Design Manager. This is the structure I have found to be most effective, based on my experience. Table 7 shows a comparison of the roles.

A programme may have its resources based in various parts of a company. Its projects are likely to be undertaken in a variety of departments, but it is useful for all members of the Programme Executive to be sited close to each other. Some programmes, however, are fairly well contained, and may be centred on one department, such as Personnel or the IT department. As the managing team, the Programme Executive should meet regularly. These meetings can form part of the scheduled cycle of meetings described in Chapter 5 (the Programme Office).

The Business Change Manager

The Business Change Manager is concerned with the change to the business that the programme brings about. Significant liaison is required, therefore, between the programme and business functions. The Business Change Manager needs to understand the requirements of each project and their contribution to the overall realisation of benefits.

The programme will bring about new ways of working, so the Business Change Manager needs to set expectations of the changes for each business function and ensure that they are prepared for the change. Conversely, local business changes need to be understood and evaluated against the objectives of the programme.

Executing this role requires a good understanding of the business functions affected by the programme. The Business Change Manager must be able to map the current business processes and articulate the benefits to senior management. The role requires great diplomacy and negotiation skills. There may be many areas resistant to change, and considerable clarity of explanation will be required when selling the benefits of change.

Consider the changes that have affected companies over the last ten years or so, particularly in working patterns. Firstly, offices gave way to open-plan areas. Then, individual desks gave way to shared desks (or *hot desks*) and job sharing appeared. Now, virtual workers are an increasing percentage of a company's workforce, with more employees working from their homes. These are dramatic changes, though few of them have ever been effected through a structured programme of change. Many have in fact crept in as incremental changes, and may not have benefited everyone equally. Having a Business Change Manager helps to ensure that all voices are heard and that the proposed changes are sufficiently evaluated for all relevant company working patterns.

One of the early activities of the Business Change Manager in the development of the programme is to establish the programme's Business Case. It is always more difficult to work from a Business Case developed by someone else, so if the Business Change Manager can be appointed at Programme Feasibility stage he or she will be able to initiate the Business Case and attain a mental ownership of it for later stages.

Some projects will need to be re-scoped during their execution, either as a result of a general change of direction or through the need to resolve a difficult problem. The effect on the programme's Business Case needs to be evaluated. Is the change merely to be deferred or is it fundamentally different?

Benefits management is a key task for the Business Change Manager. The Business Case will state particular benefits that the programme is expected to bring about, and the Business Change Manager will be looking to ensure that each completed project is actually bringing about its expected benefits. If not, he or she will need to calculate the shortfall and decide whether an additional project is needed to fill the gap.

Keeping an eye on benefits is much easier in a programme than in a single project, since the programme continues after projects have completed. In single projects, benefits management is often a diluted exercise after the project team has been disbanded. True benefits are often not realised until many months after project completion. (Chapter 7 gives more detail on this important role for the Business Change Manager).

The Design Manager

The Design Manager is an important role for managing the Programme Design. As a member of the Programme Executive, the

Design Manager has the authority to maintain the integrity of the programme design. It is important that someone at a high level in the programme can police the design, evaluating any changes to it that are proposed from the business, client, suppliers or within the programme itself.

From this purview, the Design Manager can also be the quality controller for the programme, ensuring that programme standards, procedures and product quality fall in line with design requirements. Some programmes prefer to separate quality from design and create a Quality Manager as well as a Design Manager. I have no problem with this, but, by combining the two roles in one, a significant saving in overhead can be made. In my experience, it is quite logical to combine the two roles.

In highly technical programmes, the Design Manager can be likened to a Technical Architect, and may well be given this title. For example, he or she might be an engineer, requiring a specific knowledge of safety-critical operations or systems. The role also equates to the public-sector term Design Authority.

Bearing in mind the required flexibility for a programme in terms of changes, the Design Manager needs to be able to keep a track on things like scope creep and benefits dilution. There will undoubtedly be close working with the Business Change manager on these aspects.

The Programme Design includes many aspects that need controlling, from the programme scope and organisation to programme support facilities and working space. Much of these are administered on a daily basis by the Programme Office, so the Design Manager will need to maintain a close relationship with its staff. In a large programme, the Design Manager may retain a small staff, but many programmes will be able to utilise Programme Administrators in the Programme Office to perform administrative design-management tasks.

The Design Manager can also act as a consultant to the programme's projects, assisting them to establish their own quality plans and dispensing advice concerning the management of quality. He or she may commission quality reviews and audits, as required, involving independent or third party reviewers as necessary. An initial piece of

Quality Focus	Quality Aspects
Business Requirements	*in terms of clearly stated and fully agreed requirements and statements of work*
Objectives	*project objectives, sufficiently quantified and achievable*
Benefits	*realistic, understood and achievable*
Systems	*in terms of defect-free hardware, software, etc, thoroughly tested to agreed standards by developers and users and installed to required safety standards*
Marketing and communications	*through the need to thoroughly set user expectations of what will be implemented*
Contracts	*sufficiently legal, including clear documents of understanding with suppliers and contractors*
Training	*focused on audience needs and capabilities*
Documentation	*in terms of training, support and user manuals, which are both readable and usable*
Support	*providing adequately staffed and trained Help Desks*
Project management	*providing for a properly estimated, planned and organised project through the use of reliable methodologies*

Table 6 Typical quality areas in a business and IT programme

work will be to set quality standards, to which projects should comply, and to establish an overall Programme Quality Plan.

Quality appears in many forms throughout a programme, and the Design Manager needs to have a good understanding of its many guises. Table 6 shows where quality may appear, for example, in a business programme in which information technology plays a strong role.

Testing is a fundamental proof of quality, and the Design Manager will want to ensure that individual test plans are adequate for the level of quality desired. Testing will either be ongoing for each project or concentrated in discrete test phases. Prototyping and pilots are usually discrete test phases and may have a particular effect on the Programme Design. The Design may have to be adjusted to account for problems arising during these phases.

Besides addressing quality, the Design Manager should monitor consistency of standards across projects in their scope and organisation, ensuring that change and issue control, for example, are adequately undertaken. He or she will need to ensure that dependencies between projects are mapped and that no duplication of work is undertaken.

Breaking down the programme design into manageable elements will be an early task for the Design Manager. Few software tools cater totally for design management. However, there are various change control and configuration management applications that will allow design elements to be classified as configuration items, from which changes may be tracked.

The Risk Manager

I am often asked why I suggest a specialist Risk Manager be appointed to a programme. Should not the Programme Manager be responsible for risk? My answer is born from experience. For me, the Programme Manager is accountable for risk but is not the best person to manage it. There is often a conflict of interest in the targets driving the management of a programme and the impartiality needed to focus on a programme's risk. It is easy to pay lip service to risk and adopt a tick-in-the-box mentality.

The scope of a programme, its close alignment to business strategy and the scale of change that it aims to deliver mean that risk management is an essential activity for any programme, large or small. Too often, risk management is undertaken in an amateur and half-hearted manner usually because there is no particular expertise available to accomplish it effectively. The appointment of an experienced Risk Manager at Programme Executive level ensures that risk is taken seriously and that it has a professional focus.

In performing the role, a Programme Risk Manager must be able to engage expertise in the identification and assessment of risk and to take a balanced view of its management, advising the Programme Manager of suitable risk containment and contingency plans. Expertise may be drawn from within the programme, the company or from outside of the company. The Risk Manager needs to be able to act as a consultant to each project in its identification, assessment and management of risk, offering to facilitate risk identification workshops and ensuring consistency in the risk management process.

The Risk Manager defines the risk management process for the programme and ensures that the Programme Office is able to administer the programme risk register. He or she also ensures that risks are analysed to defined programme standards and that due diligence is practised for risk throughout the projects. There is usually close working with the Business Change Manager, since the risks of making changes to a business need to be thoroughly understood.

The role is complex and can be taxing. In a technical programme, a Risk Manager may be dealing with life-threatening possibilities. If a building collapses, the architect is blamed, but the Risk Manager may also be to blame if due warning was not given.

A Risk Manager has to rely on good judgement and a good supply of precedence data, plus some sophisticated analysis techniques and metrics. Above all, a professional Risk Manager should bring deep experience. Not all risks can be avoided, but the right focus and attention can minimise their impact.

Risk management for programmes is discussed in detail in Chapter 6.

The Programme Manager

The Programme Manager is the key day-to-day management role for the programme. Those who believe a Programme Manager to be a form of super Project Manager are deluding themselves. The role has more to do with managing a business than managing a project, and represents one of the fundamental differences between project and programme. There are Project Managers who could assume the role of Programme Manager without difficulty: a knowledge of project management is certainly valuable. However, the mindset is different and would be alien to some Project Managers. If anything, the role of Programme Manager is closer to that of Project Director; neither is scheduling the detailed work of others. The day-to-day work is focused through the constituent projects and their managers.

Managing a programme is, therefore, a particular skill. Programmes are often cross-functional and cross-divisional, requiring high

Risk Manager	Business Change Manager	Design Manager	Programme Manager
• Manage risk	• Own and manage the Business Case	• Own and manage the Programme Design	• Manage the day-to-day programme
• Define and own the risk management processes	• Manage the benefits	• Manage quality and testing	• Own the programme plans
• Advise the projects on risk identification, assessment and containment	• Manage user and business expectations	• Evaluate change requests that impact on the programme	• Set personal objectives
• Analyse risks	• Prepare business operations for change	• Map project and programme dependencies	• Monitor programme objectives
• Advise the Programme Manager and Steering Group on best courses of action	• Validate business requirements		• Report progress, risks, issues and changes to the Steering Group
			• Chair programme reviews
			• Monitor the Blueprint
			• Balance programme resources
			• Negotiate resource requirements
			• Balance the budget

Table 7 Summary of Programme Executive Roles

diplomacy and negotiation skills. The Programme Manager advises, analyses and applies management techniques to the resolution of problems and the progression of plans.

In many ways, the Programme Manager is performing a balancing operation. He or she is attempting to achieve effective cost management, resourcing capacity, work efficiency, quality and risk coverage, without diluting the benefits. The objectives of the programme need to be constantly monitored to ensure that they are all adequately covered.

The Programme Manager owns the programme integrated plan, which is a rolled-up summary of each project's plan, including dependencies. This plan is used to steer the programme and is discussed in Chapter 5.

In balancing the resourcing requirements for the programme, the Programme Manager needs to be able to secure commitment from line managers and equally be able to negotiate for resource with contractors and third parties. Both aspects are subject to frustration: on the one hand there is often conflict between the programme and business operation, on the other there are questions of loyalty and staff assimilation. The efficient use of resources is a constant concern for the Programme Manager.

The Programme Manager is, therefore, reliant on timely and accurate management information. This could come from a variety of sources both from within the programme and outside it. Most should come, however, from the Programme Office, and the Programme Manager needs to carefully consider information requirements at an early stage in the programme lifespan.

Decision support software and analysis skills are costly. They need to be considered during the Programme Design stage if the budget is not to be compromised later by unplanned requirements. I have seen some unfortunate attempts to implement complicated and novel analysis tools after a programme has got under way in order to satisfy a perceived information requirement. The result was a considerable amount of time and effort spent in learning and experimentation as Programme Office staff attempted to understand the new software!

Relationship with the Programme Executive

The Programme Manager needs to form a close team with the other members of the Programme Executive. Table 7 summarises the tasks of each role. Ultimately, the Programme Manager is accountable for the day-to-day management of the programme, though the other members of the Executive are accountable for particular processes.

This is not management by committee. The regular meetings that the Executive will hold are more like opportunities to communicate progress and discuss mutual activities, rather than agreeing policy.

From the Business Change Manager, the Programme Manager needs to know how the acceptance of change is progressing. The Business Change Manager will discuss with the Programme Manager the preparation of change for particular areas. Typical questions are:

- *Have expectations been adequately set?*

- *Are departments gearing up adequately for the expected change, in terms of resources, facilities, etc?*

- *Is the amount and type of end-user training adequate?*

- *How is the take-up of training progressing?*

- *Are any of the business requirements likely to change?*

As projects complete and deliverables are implemented in the relevant parts of the company, the Business Change Manager needs to know how successful these have been. The Programme Manager may need to plan additional projects or change vehicles in order to correct unexpected problems in particular areas where projects have been implemented.

For the Programme Manager, the Business Change Manager is a vital link to the business of the company. It is through the Business Change Manager that the Programme Manager can receive intelligence on important events outside the programme.

From the Risk Manager, the Programme Manager needs to understand the risk exposure to the programme and whether risks are increasing or decreasing in particular areas. The effect of mitigation actions needs to be determined and the state of current risk reserves against eventualities. Typical questions are:

- *Is risk being actively managed in all parts of the programme?*

- *Are mitigating actions having an effect on the total risk exposure?*

From the Design Manager, the Programme Manager needs to understand progress against the Programme Design and whether proposed changes will affect the original design concept. The status of testing and deliverable quality will also need to be understood. Typical questions are:

- *What is the current status of changes?*

- *What is the status of programme dependencies and has the way they affect the programme changed?*

- *Is the desired level of quality being achieved?*

Relationship with the Project Managers

The Programme Manager needs to meet regularly with the Project Managers. This is not just to understand how each project is progressing, but to be able to give each project the advantages of economies of scale. Each Project Manager will be focused on his or her own project, but needs to understand the programme view and take advantage of common facilities. These will include:

- common planning and quality standards

- resourcing opportunities and management

- inter-project dependencies

- common risks and issues: programme resolution possibilities as opposed to individual project resolutions

- common equipment and facilities

- common communications plan

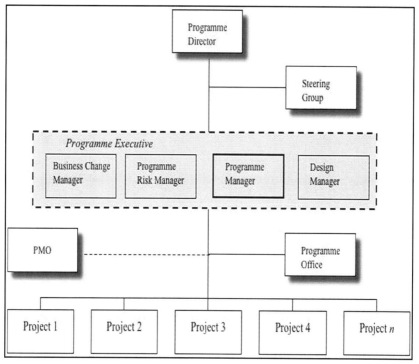

Figure 9 Typical large programme organisation

- reporting requirements

- project review requirements

Chapter 5 covers the reporting requirements from project to programme, but each Programme Manager will want to establish his or her own reporting package with the Project Managers, either formally or informally. The Programme Manager may also want to set budget tolerances for each project and suggest performance objectives.

The programme should be able to provide guidance and consultancy to each project for such aspects as risk management, project planning and quality management, via skills in the Programme Executive and Programme Office. Certainly, common project functions such as deliverables management and testing can be "packaged" by the programme to a large extent, such that projects need not have to spend significant time establishing them.

The Programme Office maintains a regular detailed link with each project, while the Programme Manager maintains a more strategic relationship.

I feel it important that the Programme Manager encourage a community of project managers. There will be many links between the projects, so it is worthwhile having project managers meet regularly to discuss those links and share information.

The Programme Director and Steering Group

The Programme Executive is usually directed by a *Programme Director*. This is often a part-time role and ensures the link between the company executive team and the Programme Executive. The Programme Director might well perform the same role for other programmes within the Change Blueprint, depending on his or her available time.

The Programme Director finds and allocates Sponsors for each of the projects commissioned within the programme and assists in the justification and priority of the projects within the overall business. The programme itself needs a Sponsor, which may or may not be the Programme Director. Large or whole-company programmes may have both a Sponsor and a Programme Director. Chapter 6 gives more information on the role of Sponsor.

In a busy programme there will be regular dialogue between the Programme Manager and Programme Director concerning such things as the direction of the programme, the resolution of issues, the containment of risks, the apportionment of funds and deployment of resources.

A key role for the Programme Director is to ensure that the programme remains in line with the Change Blueprint and Business Strategy, ensuring that the programme is accorded the correct level of priority within the Blueprint. This steering of the programme is accomplished most beneficially via a Steering Group, which is chaired by the Programme Director. The Steering Group represents key business functions (including Sponsors of current projects) plus the Programme Executive, and meets at frequent intervals, depending on the programme's priority. Monthly, six-weekly or quarterly seem to be typical intervals.

It is important to ensure that the terms of reference for the Steering Group are drawn up during Programme Design. These include the limits of its decision-making powers and the boundaries of its involvement. The Group should not become involved in the mundane management of the programme. This is the work of the Programme Manager and Programme Executive. Instead, the Group should give guidance on direction, and sanction or refuse initiatives which are outside the Programme Manager's financial or decision-making remit. The Group should also act as a channel between the programme and the business operation.

A typical Steering Group agenda might comprise:

- Programme progress to date

- Project completions and new projects to be commissioned

- Budget status

- Resourcing status

- Major programme issues

- Major programme risks

- Change requests for approval

- Actions for Steering Group approval

- Business status

Steering Group members should be fully aware of their roles. It is all too easy for the Steering Group meetings to become talking shops rather than a body for direction and sanction. I have seen situations where this has occurred. To prevent it happening, the Group needs to have something to discuss. It should not meet just for the sake of it (ie, because a meeting date has been fixed). Steering Group members will be busy, senior people, and should not have their time wasted. The Programme Director needs to ensure that there is an agenda worthy of discussion.

If Steering Group meetings are tied to a reporting cycle, then a "package" of information can be produced for information and debate. Each Steering Group meeting can then be the ultimate in a series of scheduled reviews, culminating in a roll-up of data from each project.

Governance of the programme is a key concern for the Steering Group, Programme Director and Programme Executive. These roles will require information at different levels of detail and for different purposes. Governance is described as a separate topic in Chapter 9.

Projects within a programme

The programme organisation structure is not complete without its constituent projects. Their link to the programme on a day-to-day basis is via the Programme Office (described in Chapter 5). Potential projects will be identified during the Programme Design stage, but each one will need to undergo its own separate scoping. As the programme progresses, new projects will be conceived. The Programme Office should set management standards for these projects, enabling them to fit into the programme reporting structure. In the Corporate Programme Office example of the retail finance company mentioned in Chapter 2, all projects conformed to a company standard controlled by the Programme Office. This greatly simplified the recording and reporting of information centrally and ensured that each project knew its place in the corporate strategy.

An important early task for the Programme Office is to construct, circulate and keep up to date a programme organisation chart. The organisation chart is a vital communications vehicle both for those within the programme and those outside it. Figure 9 shows a typical organisation chart for a large programme.

The Programme Manager appoints Project Managers for each project as it is it is commissioned, and the Programme Director appoints a Sponsor for each, ensuring buy-in from the business area concerned. It is important that these projects lock into the common reporting style and cycle established for the programme. Consistency of reporting (common software, house-style, accounting conventions, etc.) saves considerable time and effort, yet, surprisingly few programmes manage to achieve it. It is certainly more difficult to achieve if one or more projects are operated by subcontractors off site. It may be costly for them to adhere to say, common software standards, and so may attempt to seek a compromise. Contractual terms can, of course, specify such requirements, though in the heat of negotiation these things can be inadvertently omitted.

A question which often arises is *how autonomous can projects be within a programme?* Clearly, the programme should not attempt to establish a bureaucracy, with a Programme Office operating strict control over the day-to-day operations of each project. The Programme Manager should ensure that each Project Manager is given a wide degree of authority and accountability for his or her project, which extends to budget, resource recruitment and management, and other operational requirements. However, the Programme Executive and Programme Office are able to see the big picture and take advantage of critical mass in terms of resourcing, balancing the overall budget and managing an integrated plan, so a regular information flow from each project is a valid and essential requirement. The balance to be achieved is not to make this requirement an interference or perceived as a chore.

Conversely, there is no point duplicating project work by recording every project issue, risk and change at the programme level. The Programme Executive needs to be able to trust each project to manage its work effectively and properly, reporting only the items essential for the management of the programme. Indeed, there could be thousands of tasks at project level which would be superfluous at the programme level. In the Inland Revenue Self Assessment Programme, for example, 170 planned events were recorded at programme level, representing 160,000 tasks over 42 projects. Selection of the 170 key events was a critical success criterion for adequate programme planning.

How each Project Manager relates to the programme in terms of reporting and meetings attendance needs to be considered during Programme Design. Some projects will be of short duration, while others may last the complete lifespan of the programme. Some projects may merely be different phases of the same piece of work. Thus, any regular meeting of Project Managers and the Programme Executive may comprise different persons as the programme progresses.

A key requirement for the programme is to be able to achieve economies of scale in terms of expenditure, procurement, training, resourcing and technology. To this end, establishing project links will be an important piece of work and one that needs to be regularly maintained.

Summary
The choice of organisation and roles must depend on the nature of the programme. All roles consume cost. There will be times when a leaner organisation is appropriate and times when additional roles will need to be implemented. I would expect a programme organisation chart to be changing quite frequently. This chapter suggests a generic organisation template, which the author has used to good advantage on many occasions. It can be adapted for particular types of programme, bearing in mind the need to fulfil the important management activities described.

Project managers should be given a tolerance and authority to manage their projects without undue influence from the programme. However, establishing a community of project managers will help to maintain inter-project links, share information, facilities and possibly resources, and to develop a sense of belonging to the wider programme and its goals.

Programme organisation and design is a complex operation. The appointment of an experienced programme management consultant should ensure that the programme is established on a firm footing, and should save valuable time in the Design stage.

Chapter 5

*t*he Programme Office – Concept and Role

Purpose

The Programme Office is the programme's administrative nerve centre. It should not be confused with a company Programme Management Office (PMO). The Programme Office described in this chapter is one that directly supports a single programme during its lifespan. A PMO is a permanent function that supports company change through the implementation of standard programme and project approaches (see also Glossary). Figure 9 in Chapter 4 shows the relationship of a PMO and Programme Office to a programme. Note that the PMO is usually a dotted-line link, unless it is going to provide *all* the administrative support to a programme, in which case the Programme Office would not be required.

The Programme Office supports the Programme Executive by undertaking such activities as:

- programme reporting

- programme resourcing

- programme planning

- management of the programme risk register

- management of programme issues and changes

- control of the programme budget

- procurement of equipment across the programme

- management of programme objectives and benefits

- maintenance of standards across the programme

- administration of programme quality plans

- programme consulting

Each project within the programme is responsible for managing its own local plans, budget, risks, issues and changes, etc., and, depending upon its size and scope, may establish its own supporting administrative organisation in the form of a Project Office. While some of the projects in the programme may be small, short-lived undertakings, others may be significant in terms of resources and scope. However, in order to take advantage of economies of scale, the Programme Office may undertake certain activities centrally on behalf of the projects, such as equipment procurement.

The Programme Office must not become a bureaucratic organisation. It needs to exert control of standards across each project and compile valuable information, but at the same time it needs to be supportive, both of individual projects and Project Offices and of the Programme Executive.

Some of the activities of a Programme Office are larger implementations of Project Office tasks, but there are fundamental differences between the two functions. The Programme Office has a much wider scope and is focused as much on analysis work as purely administrative activities. Considerations such as resource utilisation, risks, funding and expenditure are considered across the whole

Project Manager's role *for the project*	Programme Office roles *for the programme*
● direct the project; be responsible for its success	● administer the programme management system and advise on process
● review and report project progress	● track and analyse programme progress; roll-up project progress
● make decisions for the containment of risk; resolve issues; approve changes	● log issues, risks and changes, and analyse at programme level
● manage resources	● prioritise programme resourcing
● validate task durations and effort	● receive data from projects and collate for overall reporting
● validate and own project plans	● roll-up and analyse project plan data
● chair project reviews	● call formal reviews
● liaise with business and third party management	● be a centre of information for the programme
● manage contractual relationships	● provide administrative support to the Programme Executive
● be accountable for the project budget; approve costs and expenses	● administer the overall programme budget
● ensure project standards are correctly implemented	● set management standards for the programme and each project
● monitor resource effectiveness	● administer programme timesheets and analyse earned value
● understand user and business requirements	● administer programme business objectives
● create team objectives	● advise on overall programme standards for team-working

Table 8 Complementary activities of a Project Manager and the Programme Office

programme, and project interdependencies play a large part in balancing these and other competing priorities.

Companies who have had experience of using a Programme Office are normally sold on its benefits. However, others may need to understand its significant advantages. The Inland Revenue Self Assessment Programme, for example, had difficulty in selling the concept of a Programme Office initially, since it was not a commonly utilised function in IR programmes, but once established it quickly gained credibility and approbation.

Organisation

Organisationally, the Programme Office supports the Programme Executive and the programme's projects, though each project may have its own Project Office. Roles tend to be a mixture of full and part time appointments. It is recommended that the Programme Office be sited close to the Programme Executive in order to receive and convey information rapidly.

As well as providing support and information to the Programme Manager and his Executive, the roles in the Programme Office need to complement the role of each Project Manager. Table 8 shows how the role of the Project Manager is complemented through activities in the Programme Office. The Project Manager directs his or her project both within the boundaries of authority and to the standards established by the programme. The Programme Office administers these standards.

The staff resources of the Programme Office will grow with the programme. As each project is commissioned this needs to be re-assessed. The Programme Office only needs to be as large as the demand on its resources.

A typical set-up might comprise:

- Programme Office Manager

- Full-time Secretary

- Planning Analysts

- Programme Administrators

- Programme Consultants

- Programme Specialists, such as a Financial Controller

In a programme that has a scarcity of project management skills, the Programme Office might also undertake or procure project management training. A methods consultant could also be employed to ensure the integrity of the management methods throughout the programme. Other consultants could be useful to coach projects in areas such as risk, budget control and planning.

The Programme Office is an excellent training ground for acquiring programme and project management skills and many organisations like to place trainee project managers alongside skilled Programme Office staff.

Figure 9 shows the position of the Programme Office in a typical programme organisation chart. If a company has a permanent, corporate, divisional, regional or functional PMO established, it makes sense for the Programme Office to link to it. The Programme Office would not want to duplicate support that a PMO might normally give to all programmes. Certainly, a Programme Office would want to align to PMO standards for programme and project management.

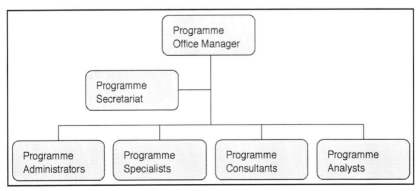

Figure 10 Sample Programme Office organisation

Programme Office Roles

The roles outlined below are representative of a typical Programme Office. Depending on the size, nature and scope of the programme these activities could take on greater or lesser significance, so that each job description may not need to equate to a single role. For example, it is quite conceivable for a *programme administrator* to also assume the activities of *systems and documentation administrator*, or a *planning analyst* to assume the activities of *methods analyst*.

Programme Office Manager

The Programme Office Manager is a senior appointment. He or she manages the day-to-day operation of the Programme Office. Ideally, the manager is responsible for setting up the office, so an early appointment in the programme's lifespan is desirable.

Typical tasks are:

• be responsible for the set-up and operation of the Programme Office

• manage Programme Office resourcing, equipment, facilities, funding

• manage Programme Office personnel, setting personal objectives and performance targets

• advise the Programme Manager and Executive of out-of-line project and programme situations

• provide management information to members of the Programme Executive in support of their control of the programme, and be accountable for the accuracy of data in monthly progress reports, etc.

• be responsible for the provision of relevant programme and project management training

• be accountable for the interpretation of the programme management system and management methods utilised across the projects

- deputise for the Programme Manager, where applicable

- forge and maintain link with any company PMO.

Planning Analyst/Consultant

The Planning Analyst plays an important technical role in a Programme Office and may be supported by one or more Planning Administrators. The Planning Analyst is concerned with the accuracy of plans and the adequate coverage of tasks by resources and effort. It is a skilled role which also involves a degree of consultancy to give advice to individual projects in their planning and estimating.

Typical tasks are:

- set and maintain standards for programme, project and sub-project planning

- advise on estimating and planning techniques and use of planning software

- run occasional training in planning and estimating

- roll up and analyse plans received from projects
  — validate task and resource estimates
  — monitor task dependencies and plan interdependencies
  — monitor milestones

- monitor project interdependencies with the Design Manager

- prepare and maintain an integrated programme plan

- report plan status

- assist with the design of programme phases

Programme Office Administrator

A programme may need one or more Programme Administrators to administer day-to-day tasks. Much of the work involves collecting data, recording it, logging it and compiling reports for the Programme Executive and Steering Group.

Typical tasks are:

- maintain programme exceptions logs and registers (risks, issues, changes)

- progress and analyse exceptions and report status

- manage the programme time-recording system

- maintain central filing for vital programme information (e.g. vendor contracts)

- collate monthly progress reports and regular information from projects

- prepare information for monthly programme report

- schedule and arrange formal project reviews

Programme Financial Controller

The Programme Financial Controller is a necessary role for any programme. The scale of programmes is usually such that they represent a sizeable investment for a company or business. In order to ensure that the programme operates to optimum cost effectiveness, the Financial Controller will be an experienced accountant, able to record and analyse costs and expenditure to a high degree of accuracy.

Typical tasks are:

- maintain programme

- validate expenses and costs

- reconcile expenses and costs

- monitor and forecast expenses and costs against and contracts

- analyse expenses and costs, report their status and compile earned value trends

- prepare financial input for the monthly programme report

Quality Administrator/Controller

The Quality Administrator, or Controller, is a role that supports the Design Manager and may or may not be sited in the Programme Office. In a small programme, the administrative aspect of the role could be taken by a Programme Administrator, and the more analytical aspect of the role could be accomplished by the Design Manager. For some programmes, however, quality is of prime importance, justifying the establishment of a separate role.

Typical tasks are:

- provide administrative support to the Design Manager

- assist in the production of the overall programme Quality Plan

- advise and assist projects in establishing their Quality and Test Plans

- schedule Quality Reviews and Project Audits

Systems and Documentation Administrator

This role may not be a full-time. In a small programme the tasks could be supported through a line operation. It is best not to be too inventive in establishing systems for the Programme Office, as there are usually enough set-up problems with the most standard of software.

Typical tasks are:

- organise electronic filing and retrieval of programme documentation

- configure Programme Office hardware and software

- set up and maintain communications links

• advise projects on systems and document management

Programme Secretariat

The Programme Secretariat may be thought of as the glue which holds the Programme Office together. The Secretariat is often the first link for information requirements from either within or outside the programme, so has a key communications role to play.

Typical tasks are:

• respond to incoming calls, and route information requests to the right persons

• support the Programme Executive and Programme Office Manager with secretarial duties

• arrange programme meetings and take minutes

• provide a filing and document production service

• arrange off site accommodation for contractors, etc.

It is easy to underestimate the size of these tasks. So many programmes set out with half a person in this role. Others try to fulfil other Programme Office roles through the Secretariat. It is important, though, not to dilute Programme Office roles merely for the sake of cost saving.

Establishing a Programme Office

In establishing a Programme Office the size, nature and scope of the programme needs to be considered. Typical questions to ask are:

• *Is the programme spread across geographical boundaries? ie, Europe, global*

• *Will communication between projects and the Programme Office be manual or electronic?*

• *Are existing electronic links in place? e.g. Email, EDI, LAN, WAN*

- *Where will the Programme Executive reside?*

- *Is there physical space for the Programme Office close to the Programme Executive?*

- *What local or networked computing exists currently?*

- *Are standards already established in the company for personal computing hardware and software? e.g. for word-processing, spreadsheets, project planning, databases*
- *Are company project management standards already in place?*

- *Are company programme management standards already in place?*

- *Are there people in the company with the necessary Programme Office skills, or will resources need to be brought in?*

- *Will the concept of the Programme Office need to be sold to a sceptical organisation?*

The Programme Office will be a busy environment. People will need physical access as well as electronic access. A Local Area Network (LAN) will be an important requirement. The Programme Executive will need regular and often instant information on the status of various parts of the programme. A half-hearted approach will only cause frustration and result in an unproductive and low quality service. The investment in Programme Office support is a significant part of the overall programme Business Case. It should not be considered an afterthought. Allowance should be made for people, computer equipment, software, telecommunications, storage space, office space, desks and facilities — all growing with the programme.

Set-up of the Programme Office should begin during Programme Design, allowing time for recruitment of staff and provision of office facilities. The Programme Office Manager is one of the key roles which should be recruited during the early part of Programme Design.

Operation of a Programme Office
Programme office tasks are generally split between administrative,

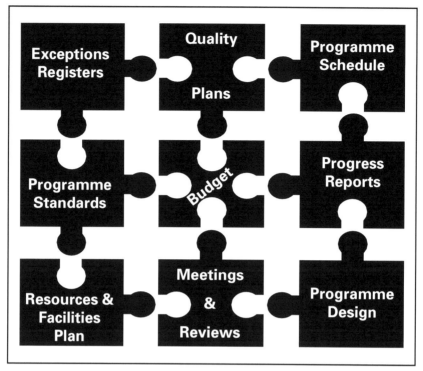

Figure 11a Typical Programme Office administrative elements

analytical and educational. The range of skill levels required, such as from secretarial to consultant, is, therefore, large.

Activities tend to centre around a need to support the Programme Executive with statistical information and a need to support each project with advice and guidance on programme standards. Day-to-day activities are concerned with collating, analysing and reporting information and advising and mentoring. Figures 11a and 11b overleaf summarise these activities. Much activity occurs on a regular cycle to coincide with the need for programme governance, which is described in Chapter 9.
Exceptional activities occur with, for example, the commissioning of a new project, when assistance will be required in setting up its standards and information protocols. Also, the Programme Office will be involved in periodic audits of projects for compliance to standards.

The information cycle
Most programmes work on a monthly cycle of reporting information. Data is submitted fortnightly from each project at summary level, and

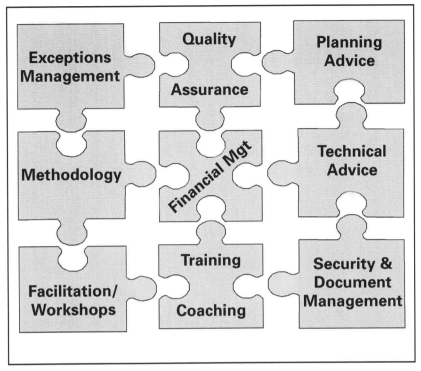

Figure 11b Typical Programme Office consultative elements

plans are rolled up into a monthly integrated programme plan. A register of projects is usually maintained, which typically records the following information:

- project name and manager

- key objectives

- key milestones

- key deliverables

- position and priority within programme

- key dependencies

- number of resources

- capital value

In addition to the register (which is largely static and does not require continual updating) is the monthly reporting package, which typically records each month the following for each project:

- current status (e.g. red, amber, green) in terms of work against schedule and costs

- current key risks
- current key issues

- major changes requested and outstanding

- a brief résumé of achievements over the previous month

- a forecast of key activity for the coming month

The monthly package will usually be supported by analyses of earned value, expenses and risks. Based upon information in the monthly package, the Programme Executive will make judgements concerning the apportionment of resources and funding across the programme, the resolution of issues and containment of risks, the approval of changes against the Blueprint and the prioritisation of projects in line with current business requirements.

Clearly, in order to be effective, each project must report information in an identical format, and plans must be submitted to consistent standards.

Exceptions management

The Programme Office needs to identify and record key exceptions from each project. These are generally risks, issues and changes, though additional exceptions may be relevant for particular programmes (eg, software errors, production errors).

A process for managing exceptions needs to be firmly established during Programme Design. This should include levels of authority and approvals needed, as well as who records what and when. In general, each project would maintain its own exceptions registers, whether it has a Project Office or not. The Programme Office acts as a high-level filter for rolling up data for analysis and reporting exceptions that are critical to the programme. It is important not to duplicate the work undertaken in this area by each project, but in practice, the Programme Office needs to be able to inspect exceptions registers in order to analyse their impact across the programme and to ensure consistency of recording. Several projects may have a similar issue or be recording the same risk. This information is particularly valuable to the Programme Office, who may be able to implement a programme wide resolution.

The Risk Manager will probably want to use the Programme Office to keep the programme risk register, and may also wish to delegate certain risk analysis tasks. If so, the results of any risk identification or evaluation sessions run by the Risk Manager can be fed to the Programme Office for inclusion in the register and subsequent analysis.

The longevity of a programme will inevitably mean changes arising from market forces, business direction, legislation, technology, etc. Few programmes complete exactly as envisaged in terms of scope and delivery. A programme, therefore, needs to be prepared for change and be flexibly structured in order to react efficiently to change. A firmly managed change management process needs to be in place, to which there is commitment from all those involved in the programme. This includes subcontractors, whose terms and conditions of engagement must bind their commitment to the process. It also includes commitment from the Programme Executive and Steering Group to honour the process and make it work, as there will be considerable pressures applied in reaching decisions on change.

With technological change, for example, which is now accelerating at a logarithmic rate, decisions about taking advantage of new technology must be well understood in terms of cost, benefit, schedule upheaval and technical stability. It is easy to be convinced that the latest piece of technology is a change for the best for a programme, but experience shows that pioneering new technology is a regular contributor to project and programme failure.

Analysis

The ability of the Programme Office to see the whole programme enables it to provide early warning to individual projects on aspects such as resourcing, costs, interdependencies and risks. Analysis of

Communication was an essential element of the Inland Revenue Self-Assessment Programme. The walls of the 'War Room' were used for up-to-date, easy-to-read charts. Hector (Inset) formed a part of the major publicity exercise to the public

plans, resource loadings, exceptions and costs allow the Programme Office to recommend approaches to the Programme Executive which will enable the programme to be more efficient and cost effective.

Access to prior data is important when analysing trends, and, therefore, the employment of analysts with previous programme experience is useful. Certain regular analyses of data will be required for the monthly reporting package. The Programme Executive needs to decide what analyses it requires the Programme Office to perform.

Typically, the programme will be looking to examine and show:

• the utilisation of resources across the programme

• earned value of work by project

• cost and expense trends (eg, payments outstanding, performance against project s)

- analysis of programme risk (construction of cause-and-effect diagrams, radar charts, risk exposure, Monte Carlo simulations, impact modelling)

- position year-to date against the Business Case (funding, milestones, benefits, business change)

- performance of work groups (eg, subcontractors) and time-recording

This is a strong departure from a typical Project Office, which has a greater administrative role. The Programme Office *War Room* (see photograph overleaf) for the Inland Revenue's Self Assessment Programme was used to display large format progress charts which greatly facilitated progress tracking and discussion. It was from here that senior Treasury officials were given progress reports.

Documentation

The programme will accumulate significant amounts of documentation. Its filing and retrieval capabilities need to be particularly efficient. The Programme Office will be responsible for maintaining master programme documentation, such as the Programme Design. Much of the material will be held on-line and will involve data sharing.

During the establishment of the Programme Office particular consideration needs to be given to:

- what data needs to be accessed and how frequently

- who needs to share what data

- who owns what data

- how data will be communicated

- how data will be rolled up from the projects (e.g. project plans, exceptions information)

- how data will be secured and backed up

- how each version of data will be controlled

Retrieval of documentation needs to be fast and convenient, so systems and applications need to be selected which can support a high retrieval performance. Too many programmes fail to consider these requirements during Programme Design, and, as mentioned previously, a costly form of fire-fighting ensues when it is realised later how important they really are.

Newly commissioned projects

The Programme Office plays a key role in the establishment of new projects within the programme, ensuring that:

- a project manager is assigned

- resources are allocated

- space is found and equipment is procured

- training is given in the management methods

- standards are established correctly in each project

Of course, guidance is required from the Programme Executive in many of these areas, but the Programme Office acts as the administrative function for ensuring new projects are welcomed aboard.

Not only will new projects be commissioned but also staff will be joining various parts of the programme from time to time. It is useful, therefore, to be able to provide a roadmap of the programme for new personnel, which includes programme objectives, an up-to-date organisation chart, facilities, processes and standards. It is essential that new personnel and subcontractors subscribe to the processes defined for the programme. Lack of consistency is one of the biggest time wasters for programmes. All too often personnel spend time trying to extract data from incompatible levels of software. A particular problem is that everyone has their own favourite brand of software application (especially planning software) and there can be fierce resistance to using anything else.

Summary

If the Programme Executive is the bridge for steering the programme, the Programme Office is the engine room. Without it the programme has no driving force.

Establishing a Programme Office is a professional job. It needs to be done well, and thoroughly (not half-heartedly) if it is to be effective. It will not be inexpensive, but it is usually consistent in its requirements, so a good Programme Office can be used again in terms of its processes and systems. It is also a good training ground for personnel. The range of roles is large and there are plenty of analytical tasks as well as purely administrative and educational tasks.

If there is an existing company PMO established, then the work of the Programme Office can be made easier by establishing a link to the PMO. Indeed, some Programme Office tasks might be accomplished centrally by the PMO.

Several consultancies now offer Programme Office design and set-up services, and many also provide Programme Office resources and systems.

Chapter 6

$\mathcal{M}$anaging Risk

The role of risk management in programmes

A programme of business change is usually a wide-ranging and lengthy undertaking, commanding a high priority and focus. The risks of scale, therefore, are already enough to differentiate it from a singularly focused project. Add to this the number of inter-relationships, the cost of resources, the risks of being closely aligned to a business strategy, and it is not difficult to envisage the importance of risk management to the overall programme.

A programme needs to make an investment in risk management. It cannot be a half-hearted affair, practised once a quarter or only at programme outset. For example, a Programme Manager has to make far reaching decisions regarding the profitability of a programme and has to balance the cost of risk reduction against the potential cost of impacts. These are difficult decisions. Reducing risk is not cheap, but neither is the cost of dealing with its impact. However, not all risks can be reduced by spending money. A certain amount of risk is acceptable: the question is how much?

In projects, the identification of risk tends to be closely focused on the work to be done, with some consideration being given to the environment in which the project is positioned. In programmes, the focus on risk in the business environment and the marketplace usually has greater significance. This is partly due to the importance a programme holds within an overall business strategy, but also to the vulnerability of a programme in today's rapidly changing markets and business priorities.

Risk management at the programme level plays an important role in strategic decision-making. Decisions concerning changes to the programme in terms of such aspects as funding, resourcing, direction, quality of deliverables, priority and timescale, frequently require a sound risk management approach. Risk management techniques can support these decisions, while promoting a culture of forward-thinking in the team through their regular use.

Risk management should play a part across all phases of a programme:

• During *Programme Feasibility* it should confirm the viability of the programme and provide the basis for judgements concerning the required investment and expected benefits.

• During *Programme Design* it should support the establishment of a firm foundation, building the confidence and assurance required to get the programme off to a good start.

• During the *operation of the programme* it should provide a sound basis for ongoing management of the total programme risk exposure, and support the requirements for problem resolution and programme changes. It should also support the successful transfer to the business of completed projects, the achievement of projected benefits and performance levels, the redeployment of resources and feedback of "lessons learned".

The programme at risk

What sort of things can go wrong in a programme? A programme is at risk from many areas, but the common factor across all its components is people: people undertaking the programme and people external to the programme (in the business, in suppliers, in customers, in government, etc.). Human failings tend to outweigh technical failings, yet curiously many programme risk registers record more technical risks than people risks. This may be because the people risks are difficult to state, or perhaps in some environments it is politic to suppress them.

The *people* risks are commonly:

Poor or no change control
caused through lack of firm sponsorship or commitment to a structured change control process

Poor commitment of resources
caused through unsound positioning within the business

Besides people risks, a programme is usually susceptible to technical and business risks. Generally, there is good understanding of the technical challenges in programmes, less so the business challenges. For example, constructing the Channel Tunnel involved enormous technical risk which was fairly well understood from the early stages. In hindsight, however, the business risk seemed to have been either poorly understood, or understood but poorly communicated, resulting in the venture regularly running out of money throughout its life cycle.

The business challenges present themselves in a few discrete ways, and there is no programme that is not susceptible to them. The difficulty is recognising their sources, knock-on effects and knowing how to manage them. For example, a project to implement point-of-sale terminals in retail outlets could well be susceptible to local, regional and corporate initiatives concerning those outlets. If, say, an initiative was being planned elsewhere in the company to rationalise the number and layout of outlets, this would have a direct impact on the point-of-sale project. This example is fairly commonplace, and I have been able to expose these so-called *collision course* projects in several companies through the use of structured risk identification workshops.

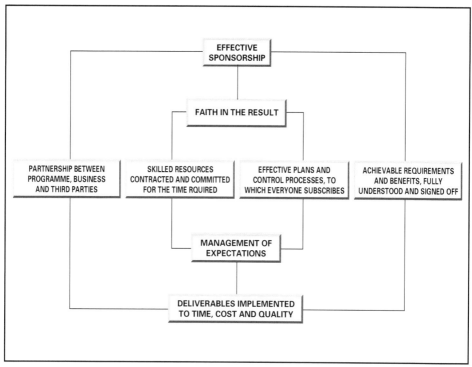

Figure 12 Eight things to get right

One of the benefits of having a PMO (see Chapter 2) is the ability to identify and prevent collision course projects from occurring.

The best way to tackle the people, technical and business challenges is through the application of good practice. Concentrating on the things to get right is a positive approach to risk and much more rewarding than just focusing on the negative aspects of risk. Figure 12 shows eight things to get right in a programme and presents them as linked requirements. Because they are linked to each other, it is necessary to establish all eight correctly in order to have a chance at achieving programme success.

These requirements can be important triggers for risk, some of which can be the causes of spectacular programme failings. They are examined in some detail in the next few pages, and can be remembered as the mnemonic **PREPARED:**

P – Partnership; **R** – Resources; **E** – Expectations; **P** – Plans; **A** –

Achievable requirements and benefits; **R** – Result; **E** – Effective Sponsor; **D** – Deliverables.

Lack of partnership

Many programmes suffer from protracted conflicts with suppliers and third parties, arising from confusion over scope and deliverables, for example, or misunderstandings concerning resources and timescales. The prime instrument in dealing with third parties is the contract. Agreeing the contract is usually the source of any conflict, and it is the thing that needs to be got right. Legally binding, it is a necessary document, but it can easily sour an otherwise good client/supplier relationship. The enthusiasm of early negotiations between a client and supplier can quickly be dimmed in protracted contractual argument.

Ideally, contracts with third party suppliers should be drawn up that allow open working arrangements. If suppliers feel the need to refer regularly to their contracts then the contracts have become a barrier to operating as a partnership.

Risk reward contracts or joint venture arrangements are preferable to standard terms for suppliers providing the major part of services to a programme. At the very least, documents of understanding should be drawn up that commit suppliers to subscribing to the management processes of the programme (i.e. the timely submission of progress reports, proper use of and commitment to the exceptions processes). Figure 13 overleaf shows the contractual divide between procurer and supplier, and suggests that a contract need not be a business barrier.

The programme cannot afford to carry conflicts of management or politics, yet every large programme seems to have its share of these. The ability to work together for the greater good of the programme, without conflict, is a challenging goal, and every Programme Manager's dream, but there are techniques which can help it along. Some of these are:

- Good expectations management, through regular and informed communications
- *Documents of understanding* between programme and business

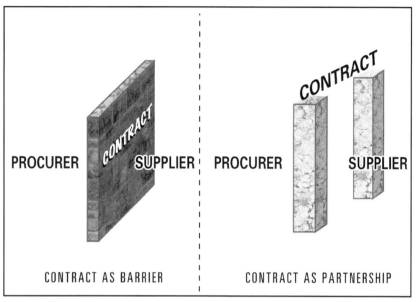

Figure 13 The contractual divide

- *Road maps* of the programme for suppliers and new starters

- Plenary meetings, associated with social events

- Team objectives and rewards

- Proper deployment of resources

- Good working conditions and environment.

Poor commitment of human resources

Often cited as the single, largest cause of project failure, the failure to commit resources for the time required is common in large programmes. It is usually a sign of inexperienced programme organisation and management.

A programme will consume large numbers of human resource, some of which will be redirected from existing business operations. This is where the conflicts usually occur, and the risks of resource decommitments are high. It is often due to poor expectation setting and conflict with line managers who can feel a lack of ownership against a programme that is currently stealing the limelight.

The Programme Director needs to establish the right priority of the programme within the lines of business and set expectations of resource requirements. Project Managers should be appointed with experience of managing project teams. Documents of understanding need to be drawn up (between line management and programme) for all projects in order to commit resources and establish their availability without ambiguity. There must be no doubt between the lines of business and the programme as to the importance and priority of committed resources' work.

Increasingly, work is contracted out to third parties. Resources are also contracted in, and effective use of this type of resource requires active monitoring. I have seen contractors whose contracts have been allowed to terminate while they are continuing to perform key roles. Uncertainties, or delays to contract renewal, cause loss of productivity. If contractors are spending time looking for their next engagement, instead of concentrating on the work in hand, then they are not being managed.

Resources can easily be lost within a large programme, and the Programme Office needs to perform capacity planning of resources across all constituent projects to ensure their efficient and cost-effective use.

Poor or unclear expectations

The construction of the Millennium Dome is a good example of unclear expectations. It is symptomatic of a "build first then decide what should go in it" mentality. Under such circumstances, how can the end result be adequately satisfied? Sponsors were expected to put up funds without knowing what they were backing. No wonder few came forward to take up the original challenges. The business expectation was that the public would view the Dome as a major construction achievement to which they would flock in vast numbers.

Expectation setting is all about marketing. It is difficult because it is subject to changes in mood and temperament of the targeted audience.

For example, in terms of engineering alone the Channel Tunnel is a marvellous feat. However, the feat of engineering was overshadowed by the enormous financial difficulties experienced, to the extent that the positive feelings of national pride it sought to exalt were soured by the many negative feelings of a project in deep financial trouble.

The overselling of expectations can be equally damaging. Expectations can be quickly destroyed by a disastrous implementation of a much trumpeted deliverable, as in the case of the new airport terminal at London's Heathrow Airport in 2008.

On a more successful note were the expectations set in the £800 million Self Assessment Tax Programme undertaken by the Inland Revenue. Here, marketing was accorded a high status in order to tackle what many might view as a negative benefit. For the Inland Revenue, Self Assessment was a vital business benefit providing considerable savings. Expectations were set using a cartoon figure named Hector, whose image as a bowler hatted gent became an icon for the programme. The important point is that the management of expectations has to be planned to reflect the benefits accruing not only to the business but also to individual employees and customers: in other words to the whole business community affected by the programme.

Chapter 7 gives a view of the importance of expectations management in the light of benefits achievement.

Ineffective plans and control processes

The managers of projects and programmes generally understand the need to establish plans and control processes, but the way in which they are utilised makes all the difference. Merely to establish processes and plans and keep records is inadequate. They have to be effective. That is, the information they contain must be of use to the general operation of the programme.

There are many examples of elegant plans being drawn up which fail to alert a Project or Programme Manager to signs of trouble. This is often because the plans are not analysed or planning analysis skills are not present. At the programme level, analysis is fundamental to the tracking operation. The business cannot afford to make decisions slowly, so accurate, up-to-the-minute management information is vital for steering the programme.

A common problem in projects and programmes is the lack of buy-in to standard processes by suppliers and subcontractors. This results in the failure by third parties to submit regular progress data and to subscribe to the common planning process. Much time is wasted cajoling suppliers for vital information or converting data from inadequate software formats. This is very much a failure by the Programme Manager in persuading suppliers to the importance of the programme and their part in its success.

The problem can also commonly extend to projects within the programme's own enterprise, and requires a strong Programme Office to ensure homogeneity of progress reporting and process management. However, the Programme Office ought not to act in a dictatorial role. Acting in partnership, it could offer expertise to projects in the compilation of their plans to standard formats.

Requirements and benefits not achievable

Chapter 7 explores the achievability of benefits, of which much also applies to the attainment of achievable requirements. Important considerations for both requirements and benefits are:

- that it is possible to achieve them

- that business and user communities comprehend them

- that they are accepted and signed-off as viable

- that a rigorous change control process exists.

However, it is often requirements which cause the most friction in programmes and projects. They are more vulnerable to change, and managing requirements change is a particular challenge for the Design Manager.

The achievability of requirements and benefits often relates to how realistic they are. "Blue sky" requirements are a venture into the unknown, often because few but the visionaries understand them. "Act-of-faith" programmes are regularly commissioned, and many have been born out of the '90s vogue for globalisation. These programmes stem from an ideal of global trading, cutting across country boundaries and traditions to create the truly international company. Few can say they have been successful, and many have cut their losses to embark on more realistic undertakings.

In the information technology sector, many projects and programmes are pioneering in nature, but enlightened organisations have learned to keep such undertakings simple and implement them step by step.

Comprehension of the requirements by all participants in a programme is vital, if their translation into completed deliverables is to be effected to the correct design. Sign-offs to design documents and acceptance criteria are also vital, and the principles of change control need to be communicated to everyone involved. I have seen ludicrous situations where a project has reached the end of its development phase and requirements have still not been signed off by the business owners.

Lack of faith in the result

The question of faith applies equally to all those who work in a programme. A determination to succeed is an important requirement not only for those at the centre but also within the projects and external suppliers. A programme whose people have faith in its outcome has a definite buzz. Teams are excited about what they are accomplishing and clearly enjoy being part of it.

When teams lose faith in their ability to deliver the change as planned, morale becomes low and productivity suffers. No amount of incentive can make up for this, and the Programme Manager needs to take regular soundings of morale across the programme.

Often, loss of faith emanates from quite mundane things. I once asked a programme team member why he was dissatisfied with working on a particular programme. He replied that the journey to work every day was stressful and fraught with difficulty and that when he arrived he was accommodated in little more than a shack! This had nothing to do with the nature of the work, which did not get a mention, but the physical environment was rated highly for job satisfaction.

Morale can vary within individual projects, and short-lived projects suffer less from poor morale than longer-term projects. Work in a long-term programme can be wearing. Some programmes have spanned several years, and ten-year programmes are not rare, particularly in the public sector. In these situations, there needs to be variety of work and a continual sense of achievement.

Ineffective or unclear sponsorship

I have mentioned the Channel Tunnel before as an example of the lessons it offers to those involved in programmes. It was not, for example, immune from ineffective or unclear sponsorship. Certainly, the government's insistence on private sponsorship meant that for the crucial early years of the programme there was no single backer or sponsor.

Without a single champion for a programme there can be no single vision. Divided visions, from many stakeholders, often mean squabbling, awkward compromises, reduced authority and longer time for decision-making.

The role of Sponsor is much misunderstood. I know of situations where Sponsors appear in name only. Many programmes aim too high in selecting their Sponsors. An effective Sponsor is not necessarily the Chief Executive, who may be far too pre-occupied to become involved in a programme. However, the Chief Executive may the ideal choice for a company-wide programme, such as Preparation for the Euro, since everyone in the company needs to understand that the change is being sanctioned from the very top. However, there is still work to do on the programme's behalf, even for the Chief Executive.

The Sponsor endorses the programme and acts as a sort of godfather. The Sponsor might appear in publicity material endorsing the programme's concepts, or the Sponsor might be the first to take delivery of an end-product and demonstrate that if it works for him or her then its good for the business. More importantly, the Sponsor champions the cause of the programme within the context of the business as a whole. If the Sponsor loses faith then the programme loses its figurehead, and its direction may be far from secure.

While a programme benefits from an overall Sponsor, each project needs to have its own Sponsor. This should ideally be a senior management appointment in the business area concerned, in order to ensure buy-in from that business. Projects that do not have such a Sponsor can suffer from a lack of commitment from their business area, which will be tested when, for example, resources are required for user testing tasks.

Deliverables not implemented to planned time, cost and quality
The trio of time, cost and quality are traditional measures of project success, but the question of whether a project is a failure if all three are not met is a question of perception. Certainly, other essential success criteria have been explored in this book, and the example has been cited in Chapter 7 of the high quality, cost effective and on-target IT solution that users could not utilise. However, even if the trio are not the ultimate criteria for project success they are strong contributors, and for many, extremely desirable.

Good planning and estimating will keep a grip on time, and good change control will ensure that "scope creep" is kept at bay. Scope creep, or the continual piecemeal accommodation of requirements outside change control, is also a contributor to run-away costs. Scope creep has been a contributory factor to the enormous differences between planned costs and actual costs in many widely reported public programmes worldwide. The key question is: *Could these costs have been forecast at planning stage, and if so, would any of these programmes have ever left the drawing-board?*

Calculating the *risk exposure* of a project or programme is a useful activity which can make a sizeable in-road to forecasting costs. The technique is described later in this chapter in the section entitled Risk Analysis. It is an attempt at calculating the total project or programme cost and is most useful in providing a contingency fund for hidden costs:

Resource costs + Equipment and materials costs + Risk exposure = **Total cost**

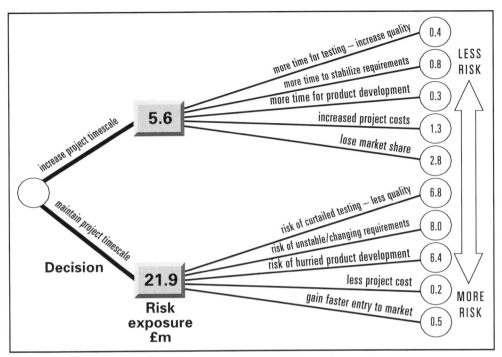

Figure 14 Example of using risk analysis for deciding the best of two options

Quality is often a product of both cost and time and is a particularly elusive goal. Many link the availability of increased time with the opportunity to increase quality, but attach a high cost to achieving quality. Of course, the perception of quality as requiring high cost is false, since quality is merely the meeting of expected standards. The old adage that "the best things are achieved with time" may have some truth, but there is usually a limit to the amount of testing that any project can undertake, when a decision has to be made that the right quality standard has been reached.

The classic project dilemma of whether to increase project time to accommodate increased time for testing or to release the deliverables as completed can only be resolved by analysis of the contributing factors. Figure 14 shows how a risk analysis approach can provide suitable options for making this type of decision. It shows the risk exposures calculated for a product deliverable, in this case a new mobile phone product, and the choice between launching the product early to achieve competitive edge, or delaying launch until further

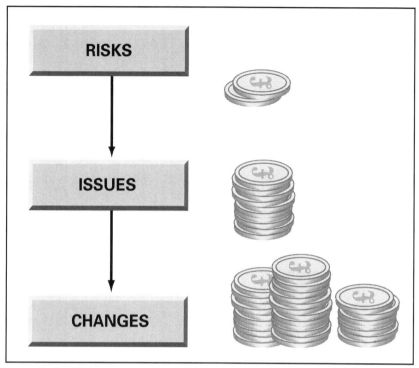

Figure 15 The link between exceptions and the relative cost of dealing with each

testing had been carried out. The pressures by the business on the project team for the former option were considerable, but the result shows the latter option carried the least risk, even though the margin of error in calculating the risk exposures was great. Only the summary risk factors are shown for each option.

Establishing risk management

The appointment of a Risk Manager will ensure that risk management is firmly established within a programme. A skilled Risk Manager can advise on the establishment of risk registers and supporting software as well as the approach to be taken for identifying and containing risk across the programme.

Each project will need its own risk register as well as one at the programme level. It is important, however, not to take the management of risk out of context. Risk is as much a programme exception as is an issue or change. If a risk impacts it becomes an issue, requiring urgent or immediate attention. Often some sort of

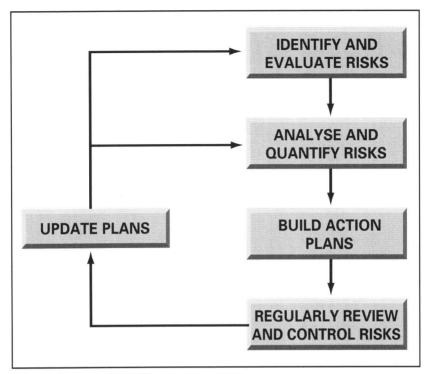

Figure 16 Summary of the risk management process

change is required to resolve the issue. Risk management is, therefore, the ability to forecast potential issues and take appropriate early action, avoiding the need for costly changes. Figure 15 shows the link between programme or project exceptions and the relative cost of dealing with each type.

Choosing software that can manage all three exceptions is preferable to holding separate registers. This ensures that exceptions are managed relative to each type, and that the factors common to each type, ie, *actions*, are appropriately applied and monitored.

The Risk Manager will probably establish a process similar to that summarised in Figure 16, and offer assistance to each project in accomplishing it. To undertake risk management well is no easy task. It is easy for any project to lapse into a state of routine "lip service" for the programme. The Risk Manager needs to ensure that the process is simple to operate and that each part of the programme sees real value in subscribing to it.

Risk No.	Area affected	Cause	Risk	Impact	Impact Cost £K	Risk Exposure £K
R0602007	Programme resources	Because User Testing falls during the peak holiday period	there is a risk that key skills will not be available for testing	resulting in a delay to delivery of the core IT projects.	5.0	2.0

Prob. %	Impact %	Date Raised	Risk Owner	Time Window	Priority	Risk Status	Evaluation comments
40	5	01/03	Vincent Johnson	3 mths	Med.	ACTIONED	Insufficient user participations during testing will result in a lower quality test, which is not acceptable. Previous testing overran through user skills non-availability.

Action No.	Mitigation Action	Actionee	Priority	Due Date	Reduction in Prob.%	Reduction in Impact	Cost £K	Action Status
A0102-012	Secure commitment of required skills for specified dates.	CDM	1	15/03	-40%	-5%	0	15/03 : Done. All but 4 resources will be available.
A0102-013	Discuss implications of re-scheduling testing with sponsor.	PR	1	15/03	0%	0%	0	15/03 : Done. Implications documented.
A0101-014	Secure 4 external resources.	CDM	2	28/03	-30%	-30%	120	28/03 : Negotiations proceeding.

Table 9 Sample page from a programme risk register

The process employed must be able to support the necessary decisions required for risk by the Programme Executive. These include whether to accept a risk and its consequences, whether to allocate funding and resources to contain a risk, whether to provide contingency, whether to avoid a risk by working round it or whether to mitigate the consequences of impact. At the programme level these are solid business decisions, so the base data must be presented in a format that favours such decisions. For example, an analysis of the distribution of risks on the risk register is of less value to a Programme Manager than an analysis of the cost benefit options of tackling the risks.

Table 9 shows a sample page from a programme risk register. This shows a single risk, its evaluation and actions to date. Importantly, it shows the risk exposure (see next section: Risk analysis).

It will be helpful to establish suitable categories for the identification, assessment and analysis of risk. This will depend on the nature of the programme and its constituent projects. Table 10 shows an example of categories established for an in-house project to upgrade point-of-sale terminals in retail outlets as part of a wider programme of change. The categories help to package risk, providing a means to concentrate on a particular area. For risk identification, the categories help to concentrate thought. For risk assessment, the categories help to channel expertise: experts can concentrate on just their field of expertise. For analysis, graphics can be constructed to compare risk in categories against particular project phases: too much risk in the Systems Testing category at project outset is less of a worry than too much during systems development, for example.

The Risk Manager will establish the number and type of risk reviews needed throughout the programme, leading regular group risk identification and risk assessment sessions. He or she will ensure that the relevant expertise is brought in to advise on the mitigation of particular risks. Often I have heard team members describe a risk as out of their sphere of involvement, exclaiming it to be a business risk

Hardware	Technical design	Software development	Systems testing
Installation sites	Schedule	Budget	Resources
Network	Training	Support	Documentation

Table 10 Example of risk categories

and so nothing they can do anything about. At the very least, the Risk Manager would have the ability to ensure that these types of risk are adequately dealt with.

Risk analysis

Risk analysis is an important undertaking for a programme, and is a sophisticated skill. So much so that the Risk Manager ought to devote a considerable amount of time to analysis work. A good Risk Manager can save a programme significant costs, by predicting issues and recommending avoiding action. Nonetheless, such expertise does not come cheaply, and is in particular demand.

The most important measure that needs to be calculated for a programme is its *risk exposure*. This is a measure of cost, which is particularly important when programme changes need to be considered. The cost of risk needs to be weighed against the perceived programme benefits. So many managers fail to take into account the cost of risk when valuing their projects or programmes. Even in cases where it is considered, the cost of risk is often an arbitrary percentage added to the programme cost for good measure. Yet there are simple ways in which the cost of risk can be calculated, and for very little effort.

A useful technique for calculating a simple risk exposure (£RE) is to estimate the cost of impact (£IC) and multiply by the percentage probability (%P) of the impact occurring. (The cost of impact is an estimate of the impact repair cost). To this is added the cost of carrying out any actions (£CA). The resulting risk exposure is effectively the insurance premium that needs to be set aside in the event of the risk occurring:

$$£IC \quad X \quad \%P + £CA = £RE$$

Figure 14 shows how the calculation of risk exposures can be an aid to decision-making.

Estimating the cost of impact is usually subjective, but since many impacts result in things such as project delay, it is possible to estimate the cost of delay without undue difficulty. In the risk example shown in Table 9 the cost of impact would represent the cost of keeping resources on the project for the delayed period, i.e. £5K. It is also

Project	Phase	Start Date	Estimated Completion	Budgeted Cost £K	£K Risk Exposure	Total Cost £K
IT5 – Network performance	Post-Contract	21/10/2005	15/03/2006	17.2	12.8	30.0
IT6 – Server enhancements	Implementation	09/07/2005	12/10/2005	35.4	22.0	57.4
IT7 – Billing	Development	09/07/2005	03/12/2005	27.1	18.0	45.1
Order process	Design	10/09/2005	01/03/2006	20.2	3.5	23.5
Web marketing	Design	24/09/2005	01/02/2006	12.0	1.8	13.8

Table 11 Sample log of projects within an e-commerce programme

shown as a percentage (Impact %) of the total cost of the programme (5%), which works out at £100K.

The value of being able to show the risk exposure for each project within a programme is immense. Table 11 shows a simple one-line log of projects within an e-commerce programme. It is immediately noticeable which projects are carrying dangerously high risk exposures in the context of their phases.

Project IT5, for example, is carrying significant risk at project outset, much of which may reflect the uncertainty of the work to be undertaken. Project IT6, however, has all its risk back loaded. It would be interesting to know whether its risk exposure at project outset was also high and, if so, whether it was signed off on the expectation that the risk would decrease. By comparison week by week or month by month, such a chart reveals a great deal about the potential cost overrun of projects. If the risk exposure trend from each project outset is also shown, together with the earned value of each project, the chart becomes an even more valuable reporting tool.

Valuable risk management techniques for use at the programme level that can assist the decision-making and forecasting process include *soft systems thinking* techniques (ref. chapter: Using Soft Systems Thinking for Programme Management), *decision trees* and *cause-and-effect diagrams*. Examples of these latter may be found in my book *Managing Risk for Projects and Programmes*.

It is both possible and desirable to take a whole programme view of risk. The opportunity to save containment costs presents itself by taking a wide view of risk across a programme's projects. The wider picture presents a different view of how risks can be mitigated or contained from that seen at the project level. However, it is reliant on being able to roll up relevant data from each project and quantify that data in order to form opinions. Some options available are:

- compare risks of a similar nature in order to understand causes and effects

- prioritise containment actions to maximum effect and cost benefit for the programme

- recommend the re-alignment of work packages or project scopes in order to avoid interdependent risks.

Summary

The key messages are:

- Risk management at the programme level is on a different scale to that at the project level, and therefore, requires particular approaches.

- A successful programme makes an investment in risk management and uses it to positive advantage, making it an inherent part of the programme management process.

- There are eight things to get right in order to reduce risk, memorable as the mnemonic PREPARED.

- Putting a value on risk and calculating risk exposures enables a better understanding of the real cost of programmes.

Chapter 7

*b*enefits Management

Benefits management is an operation that spans the entire lifespan of a programme, and is crucial to the attainment of programme success. Surprisingly, though, it is rarely given the attention deserved, and it is rarely undertaken properly.

The practical management of benefits seems to be difficult for many programmes, and may be due to a lack of understanding of the contributors to benefits achievement and the techniques available to manage benefits.

Lack of benefits management is often a root cause of programme failure, but equally damaging is poor benefits management, which attempts to manage benefits without recognition of the contributors to success. The task is, therefore, complex, and demands a wide span of control.

Unlike a project, a programme has a greater opportunity to realise benefits, owing to its longevity. In a project, benefits usually do not become apparent until some time after the project has been completed. Projects, therefore, deliver only the capability to achieve benefits. In a programme, benefits often accrue during its life. Because projects are commissioned and decommissioned throughout a programme's life, there is time for the benefits of those projects to be realised and for the programme to be re-tuned if necessary to take account of any benefits not realised.

In terms of method, benefits management usually comprises:

- the identification of benefits

- the establishment of measurable success criteria

- comprehension of the key contributors to benefits achievement

- the monitoring of expectations, requirements, deliverables and quality

- establishing benefit metrics

- the measurement of the achievement of benefits against established success criteria and metrics.

The sections that follow describe these tasks. Benefits governance is described in Chapter 9.

Identification of benefits

The benefits of a programme usually emerge from the *Business Strategy,* and should be summarised in the *Blueprint for Change*. At the Business Strategy stage, however, benefits are very much a perception of what might be achievable, and need to be properly quantified before they can move from being mere requirements. The Blueprint for Change apportions the desired benefits to relevant change vehicles (see Chapter 3), and each change vehicle needs to undergo some sort of feasibility assessment. Within a programme, this is a discrete stage – *Programme Feasibility* – and the point at which its apportioned benefits need to be validated and quantified.

The vital preparatory work for benefits management, therefore, should be conducted during Programme Feasibility. Later, during Programme Design, a benefits management method should be approved. Thereafter, the work involves monitoring and measuring the achievement of benefits as projects are decommissioned and their deliverables transferred into the business.

If only it were as simple as that! In practice, there are many things which work against the achievement of perceived benefits, such that they become diluted or radically changed, and compromise becomes a much employed option. The problem is that benefits management cannot be broken off as a stand-alone piece of management. It is bound up with deliverables management, quality management and expectations management. Benefits accrue from deliverables, which are acceptable to the business dependent upon an expectation of their quality and business improvement.

Various methods can be employed to identify and quantify programme benefits, from extrapolating from achievable goals to projecting forwards from deliverable sources. Figure 17 is a *systemigram* or *conceptual map* that gives an example of how mapping contributors to end-goals can assist the identification of benefits. It shows contributors as actions, subsequent events, assumptions and end-goals. (For the key to the shapes refer to the chapter *Using Soft Systems Thinking in Programme Management*).

This approach can test the solidity of goals through the mapping of a complete pathway, or not, to their realisation. Those goals with weak or few contributors may not be realistically achievable. The density of the mapping is up to the individual, but quite revealing charts can be produced using only summary information. Refer to the chapter *Using Soft Systems Thinking in Programme Management* for more information on this approach.

It is important to distinguish between the end-benefits and interim benefits that may be achieved along the way. As the map is built up, interim benefits may be revealed that had not previously been thought of. They might be by-products of executing particular initiatives. Figure 17 shows some interim benefits, such as "improved sales forecasting" and "lower cost invoices", leading to end-benefits. Many of these interim benefits may be designated as projects within the programme.

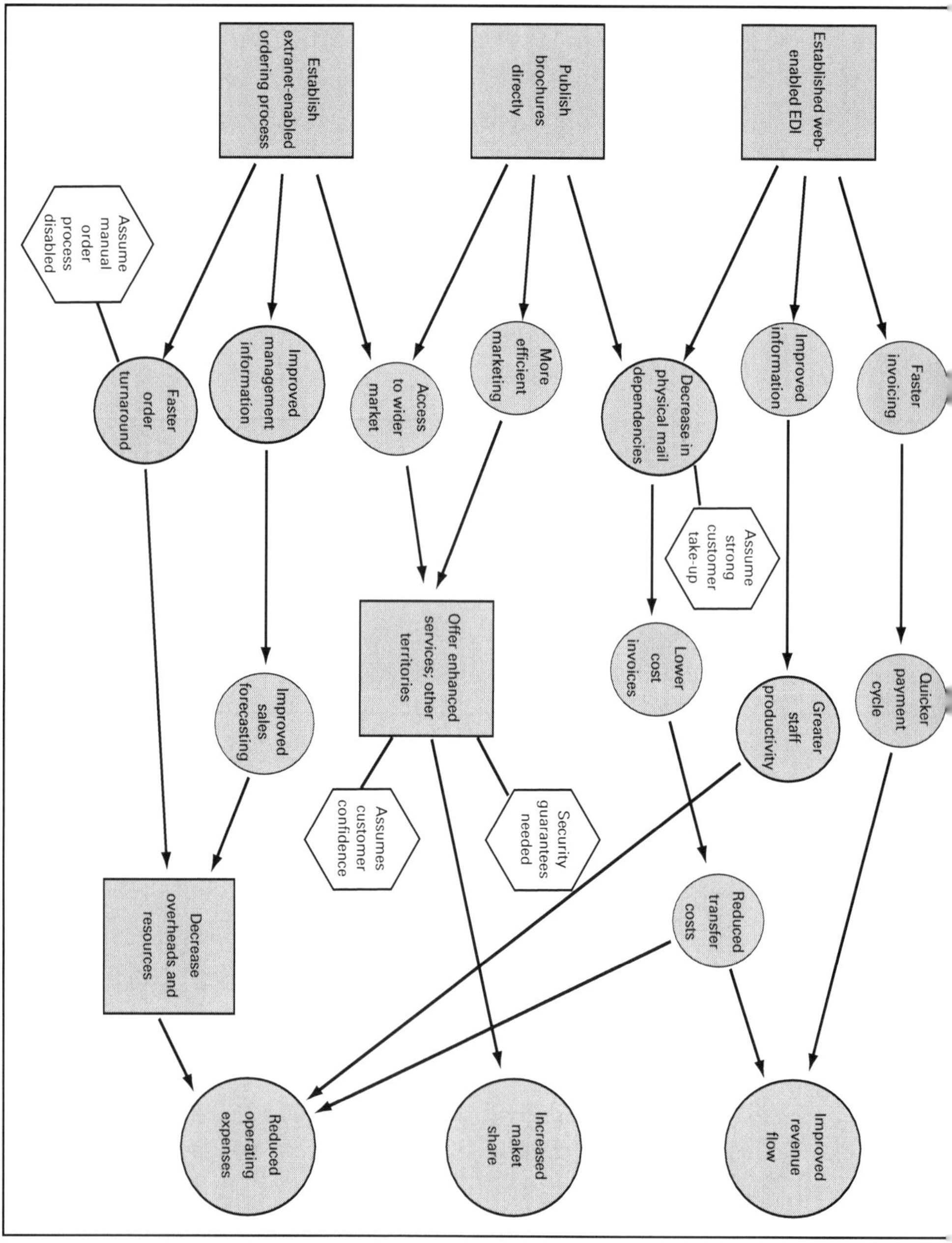

Figure 17 Benefits systemigram for part of an electronic commerce programme

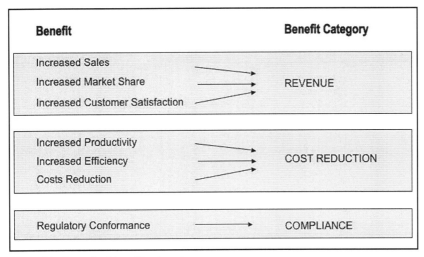

Figure 17a Example of benefit categories

It may be helpful to establish the category of benefit, so that adequate metrics may be applied. Figure 17a shows some common examples of benefits and the categories to which they belong.

Once benefits have been identified it is important to be able to quantify them. Without quantification there can be no ability to measure their achievement. (Refer to the section *Measuring the achievement of benefits*, below).

Establishing benefit metrics

If a benefit cannot be measured you cannot easily prove that it has been achieved. Establishing metrics enables the Business Change Manager to control the progress of benefits achievement.

Establishing metrics will be easy or difficult depending on the benefit category. Revenue and cost savings, for example, may be measured through existing company metrics, but compliance, employee productivity and process efficiency may need to be established by the programme.

Establishing measurable success criteria

The measure of success for benefits is their acceptance by the business against expectations articulated in the Business Strategy. Simple in concept, but often difficult to achieve in practice.

Success, like quality, is a perception. It means different things to different people. To say a programme is successful depends on a person's perspective. To some people, there is success in programmes commonly held up to be failures. For example, the construction of an innovative software program might be perceived as a success by programmers and technicians, but if it does not do what its users want it to do then it could obviously be viewed as a failure.

A programme must, therefore, establish measurable *success criteria* for its deliverable elements, and this work should be accomplished during Programme Feasibility and endorsed during Programme Design. Success criteria must state quite clearly how a particular project or deliverable will be deemed a success. Examples of success criteria are:

1. An acceptance of the new way of working by employees, measured by the complete cessation of the use of manual process 457, and an increase in productivity of 25%

2. A reduction in calls to the XYZ help desk of 15% for XYZ-related problems

3. The winding up of the XYZ administration function within 18 months of programme completion

4. The transfer of 200 employees from the outsourced ABC function to the new company within 9 months of project ABC completion.

Many success criteria are cost or productivity related (cf. sc1, above). Others are quality related (cf. sc2).

Some programmes have been perceived as bringing no benefits, since they *have* to be undertaken. These might be infrastructure projects or those which need to comply with new government legislation. *Year 2000* and *Preparation for the Euro*, for example, have both been perceived as zero benefit programmes, though some might say that the very act of making the changes must be of ultimate benefit. The

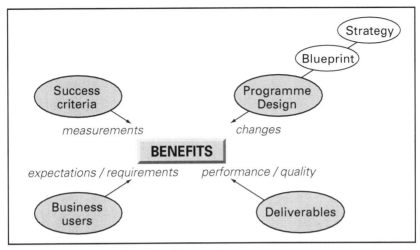

Figure 18 Contributors to benefits achievement

benefits are often difficult to quantify, however, and end up being quoted as fairly intangible things, such as "to remain in business" or "to be able to trade in Eastern Europe".

The success criteria may need to be incorporated into the test plans for the programme. The Design Manager would need to understand what forms of test would be relevant.

Understanding the key contributors to benefits achievement

It is not enough to merely specify the benefits to be achieved and their success criteria. Many actions during the life of a programme will affect the nature and quality of desired benefits.

Figure 18 summarises the key contributors to benefits achievement, and Chapter 6 highlights the risk of having unachievable requirements and benefits.

The first of the key contributors are programme changes. A programme is designed for change, so it should be expected that changes could have a knock-on effect on its benefits requirement. The Design Manager has a responsibility to ensure that change requests are examined for all possible effects, including benefits. In this respect, he or she would discuss change situations with the Business Change

Manager, who will evaluate the risks to the benefits requirement.

The Business Change Manager will also be looking to understand the progress of other contributors from the Design Manager, such as the quality and performance of deliverables. These contributors can significantly affect the required benefits, either by diluting or augmenting them. A project test phase, for example, can produce problems which could mean that the quality of certain deliverables can not be attained as originally desired, thus diluting the benefits. Conversely, the need to find alternative ways of producing a deliverable might actually augment the quality of a deliverable at no additional cost, thus augmenting the benefits. Project test phases and Quality Assurance Reviews are important activities for the Business Change Manager in benefits management. Close liaison with the Design Manager during these activities will be necessary.

How successful test phases are will affect the measurement of the success criteria. Any change to the success criteria is effectively subject to change control, since it will impact deliverable performance, quality and testing, and, therefore, benefits.

Finally, the business users themselves will have expectations of what the benefits will be, against their requirements. These need to be continually monitored by the Business Change Manager against programme activities that may affect them. In this context, it will be helpful for the Business Change Manager to compile a map of key benefits and their dependencies. Many dependent actions will occur at particular times during a programme's life, so the map could include trigger points to alert the Business Change Manager of a possible impact to benefits.

Monitoring expectations, requirements, deliverables and quality

The management of benefits in a programme is the especial concern of the Business Change Manager. If, for resourcing reasons, this role is not implemented, then the management of benefits falls to the Programme Manager and Programme Director. This is not desirable, though, since benefits management needs a strong focus, and the Business Change Manager role is ideally suited to this task through its focus on expectations setting and preparation for change.

Date	Communication	Audience	Project	Milestone	Vehicle	Test
01.05.2002	New office layout	All of Customer Orders Dept	Premises	Initial design	Display in coffee lounge	User reaction; prepared response sheet; web responses
15.06.2002	User reaction	Selected users from responses	Premises	Initial design	Divisional magazine	Interviews; editorial

Table 12 Example of summary activities from a Communications Plan

The Business Change Manager will monitor the progress of benefits against the benefits stated in the Programme Design, taking into account the success criteria specified. Any shortfalls or unexpected benefit enhancements need to be noted. Any differences can be debated by the Programme Executive.

For all this to work, though, there must be real authority vested in the Programme Executive. To soldier on, knowing that a benefit is not going to be achieved and not feeling empowered to recommend a programme change, is a failure of command. The value of benefits *will* change over time, not least during the life of the programme. It is important, therefore, to be able to have the authority to steer the programme to maximise benefits achievement.

Monitoring user expectations and requirements is a busy task for the Business Change Manager. He or she will be regularly testing user perception of the programme. It needs a good knowledge of the affected business areas and the Business Change Manager needs to be on good terms with individuals who are important to the acceptance of the change.

A Communications Plan will help the Business Change Manager market the programme to the user community and establish a process for capturing user views and ongoing requirements. The Communications Plan will show what needs to be communicated to whom and when. Table 12 gives an example.

In some cases it may be possible to prototype deliverables, as shown in the first entry in Table 12. Prototyping is an excellent opportunity for testing existing expectations and setting future expectations. As much user involvement as possible in all forms of testing is advocated in order to retain user buy-in.

Measuring the achievement of benefits

As projects are decommissioned, there is an opportunity to capture formally any lessons learned. The Business Change Manager will want to know how several things, including, but not exclusively:

- how successful was the communication of progress to the business?

- how successful was the testing of deliverables against desired quality and specification?

- have all deliverables been implemented as planned or with what changes?

- how has the business environment changed during the course of the project?

This information, together with the success criteria and original benefits statement will help the Business Change Manager decide the baseline for the measurement of each project's subsequent benefit.

It is important to know the expected time span for the achievement of benefits. Are some benefits expected to be achieved immediately upon implementation of a project or are some expected to accrue over a period of time, and if so, what period? I remember when IBM was implementing a programme in the early 1980s that delivered email and word processing capability to its UK staff. Many of the benefits were perceived as productivity gains. Measurements were taken for at least two years and the achievements regularly published to the workforce.

Measurements of productivity are notoriously difficult to obtain, and it is important to gain a consensus of how productivity will be measured. For example, considered thought will be needed in defining success criteria for a benefit claiming a workforce productivity increase of 20%. Existing measurements of productivity need to be well known, with agreed accounting conventions, otherwise there will be no obvious baseline against which to measure an improvement. A key question, therefore, for the Business Change Manager at Programme Feasibility when benefits are being proposed is to ask: "Can this benefit be measured?".

Consider a programme that aims to reduce the number of project failures in its project management community. The benefit is the reduction of project failures by 25%. Several projects and initiatives have been devised to contribute to the achievement of this benefit. One of these is the development of a "lessons learned" database, so that project managers may append their experience and retrieve it for re-use on other projects. How can this project be measured in terms of success criteria and benefit achievement?

Firstly, the benefit itself needs to be clarified. What is project failure? One could express the benefit as "the reduction of project cost overruns by 25%", which would make it more specific. Some measurements for success criteria might be:

1. The percentage of "lessons learned" from completed projects, appended to the database.
2. The number of times the database is searched by project managers per month.
3. The number of projects overrunning on cost during a 12-month period.

Others could be defined. Note that the measurement closely linked to the benefit itself (no.3) would not be appropriate on its own. Project cost overruns could have diminished in their own right without any assistance from the database. Measurement 3 needs measurements 1 and 2 to prove that use of the database is contributing to the benefit.

What can go wrong?
Many of the things that can go wrong in a programme in terms of benefits are to do with expectations management, and Chapter 6 cites this as a common source of programme risk.

A key hindrance to the achievement of benefits is company culture, and some attention to this is given later in this chapter. The culture of a company and its existing business base are powerful influences for or against the successful achievement of benefits. Culture is a particular challenge, especially since it is unusual for company culture to be taken into consideration when deciding the potential benefits at programme inception. Benefits are, therefore, often assumed to be achievable in spite of a particular company culture.

Another problem is that benefits might not be correctly translated from the Programme Feasibility document to the Programme Design, causing their potency to be diluted. The method for managing them may also not be adequate, such that they are not properly quantified or linked to programme deliverables. More commonly, benefits are the victims of programme longevity, and their perception changes within the business. This is very much the result of inadequate expectations management.

Programmes of business change are more difficult environments for the successful achievement of benefits than programmes which construct something brand new. The former can encounter continual resistance to change, since existing processes and ways of working (which staff might perceive to be totally adequate) will end up being changed. With the latter, resistance usually comes only at the planning stage.

There is also often a technical difference. For example, *e-commerce* programmes are relatively simple technically, but difficult to manage, since they change the business base. Conversely, construction of the Millennium Dome was technically difficult, but simpler to manage, since there was no existing construction to work round.

Change is a very fickle phenomenon. On the one hand, some people complain there is too much at any one time; on the other hand, some complain there is not enough. Often, in order to change something for the better, something has to get worse. This has been a common complaint against information technology, where, for example, the replacement of a complex mechanised process has often meant that the first releases of the new process are not able to perform all the tasks that the original process could do (it being too difficult, too risky or too costly to make all the desired change in one go). Consequently, the users complain of their missing function, but the technologists laud their own wisdom in not implementing too much change at once: another example of the difficulty of managing benefits when changing an established base.

This differing perception of benefits is a common cause of dissatisfaction. Those planning the implementation of programmes of business change need to understand these differences at the outset, together with their implications. A good example is the current popularity of decreasing office space by enabling a mobile workforce. Here, executive management perceives a very real saving in the size of premises against a relatively low cost implementation of laptops and communications facilities. The perception from the users of such technology, however, is very different. They perceive a major change to their working habits, and often receive poor expectation setting of the benefits. Not surprisingly there is conflict. Often the technology does not work as expected, and the very real needs of the mobile workforce have not been thoroughly investigated. The prime business reason for this considerable change is usually to save on valuable office space, but is that enough for the disruption required?

The balance between *too much change* and *not enough change* is difficult to manage. Would the worker who longs for his ageing personal computer to be replaced (*not enough change*) be willing to accept a brand new, state-of-the-art laptop and the mobile working pattern that goes with it (*too much change*)?

Managing expectations is, therefore, an art. It requires in-depth reasoning, great powers of persuasion and argument, diplomacy and subtle negotiation. Few organisations plan for this in their programmes – yet this is the role of the Business Change Manager!

Mapping the culture

A useful preliminary task that the Business Change Manager can carry out is the mapping of an organisation's culture. It is particularly relevant where an organisation's culture has caused problems previously in the implementation of change, and will equip the programme with the necessary information to manage the transition between the current business state and the projected business state. Understanding an organisation's culture will enable the rate of change to be sympathetically adjusted. It will also provide a gauge for determining the support or opposition to the proposed change. However, the mapping is best done before the programme is even conceived, i.e. at Business Strategy stage, since there can be a better gauge at this point for

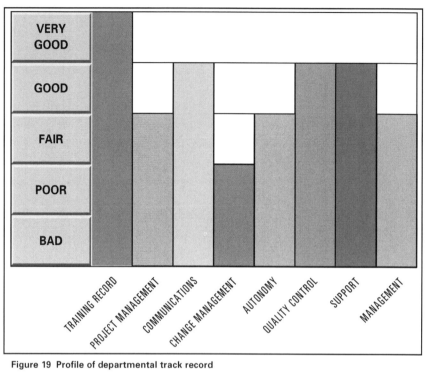

Figure 19 Profile of departmental track record

determining whether the proposed change may ever be accepted by the workforce.

Several programmes have been the victims of culture in recent years. The merger failure of the two consultancy companies, KPMG and Ernst and Young, was cited as being caused by a " clash of cultures", and many other major companies have struggled with cultural issues in their mergers and take-overs. What a shame that culture maps were not seriously considered by many of these companies prior to serious decision-making.

Culture or *"the way we do things round here"* can be mapped either for the whole company or department by department. We often talk of the *Civil Service culture* or the *retail mentality*, but what are the characteristics of these cultures? A culture's characteristics can be mapped to state whether, for example, it is rule based, risk averse or risk taking, aggressive or defensive, team based or individualistic, creative, caring, competitive or restrained, dynamic, pioneering, autocratic, etc.

Against these characteristics can be asked questions which concern various operational aspects, for example:

- Has the company a good track record in embracing change?

- Is project management a strong discipline within the company?

- Is the company regularly embarking on high-risk ventures?

- Does the company subscribe to total quality management, and is the company certificated to ISO 9001 standard?

- Is the company viewed as a "hire and fire" organisation?

- Is the company viewed as "lean and mean"?

- Is the company used to developing its own ideas or used to bringing in external expertise?

- How autonomous is each division?

- How supportive is management?

- Is there a strong track record of training?

- Is meetings discipline good?

- Is individual performance measured?

- Are communications viewed as good?

There are specialist consultants who have developed profiles for mapping culture, but simple models can be readily developed in-house, using such attributes as attitudes, power, levels of authority, decision-making, risk taking, education, skills, values, lifestyles, etc. Figure 19 gives a simple example.

For the Business Change Manager, the key questions which need to be set against a cultural response are:

- What is the state of contentment with the current operation and processes?

- What resistance to change might be expected, from past experience?

- What is the general approach to training and learning new things?

- Who in the business operation will actively support the change or who will resist it?

- Whose buy-in to the change is critical?

- What politics are at work?

There are, of course, other considerations. The Business Change Manager does need to have a view of the total company environment, since the programme could be at risk from competing initiatives, a changing marketplace, new products and services, changing technology, etc.

Summary

Benefits management is a serious undertaking within a programme. It is difficult to accomplish because benefits are often difficult to quantify. Recognition of the contributors to benefits achievement will help to focus on the things to get right. Many of these are bound up with risk management, and the same cause-and-effect type of techniques employed in risk management can be used to identify and map benefits achievement.

The role of the Business Change Manager is important for benefits management. Benefits have to be actively managed. They do not accrue automatically. Monitoring and measurement of their achievement are essential to avoid benefits dilution, loss of quality, or, more extremely, loss of appropriateness.

Chapter 8

*U*sing *Soft Systems Thinking* in Programme Management

This chapter shares some of the author's experience in using Soft systems thinking to create change blueprints, benefits maps and risk pathways for business change programmes.

Enlightened management consultants have for a number of years believed that in order to solve business problems in the "real world" it is necessary to enter a "conceptual world". In a conceptual world there are no constraints, only those limited by the imagination. Business models can be produced that show the pathways to major change. These models can then be compared to the current business state in the real world and the differences identified. With the addition of real-world constraints the model's feasibility can be tested. Programme management is a very receptive ground for such modelling. Strategic thinking is a fundamental requirement for the planning and design of programmes.

Pioneering work in this field of modelling was undertaken by Professor Peter Checkland of Lancaster University and the term *Soft systems thinking* was coined for the techniques utilised to solve "soft" problems, such as business change. Readers interested in the detailed application of the techniques are recommended to read Brian Wilson's book *Systems, Concepts, Methodologies and Applications* and Peter Checkland's *Systems Thinking, Systems Practice* (see Bibliography).

For programme management, the techniques offer the ability to construct structured business goals in the form of *root definitions*, plus conceptual models of the strategic direction of a programme or risk consequences.

Strategic mapping

Figure 20 shows an example of a conceptual map of a programme blueprint. The programme is concerned with making strategic changes to a services business. The map, reading from left to right, shows assumed pathways from a business strategy to perceived goals. The goals are quantified, but their full description is not shown. The map is built up using group planning sessions, where members of the business contribute their assumptions of the actions and outcomes needed to get from the strategy to the goals. The squares are actions or initiatives. They lead to outcomes of the actions or sub-goals (circles). They lead in turn to either further actions (squares) or directly to further goals. Actions leading to actions are disallowed. All actions need a stated outcome. Various assumptions may be made concerning the actions or outcomes, and these are represented by hexagons.

Using this simple approach (pioneered by DMR Consulting Ltd. from the work of Lancaster University and described in the book *The Information Paradox* by John Thorp [see Bibliography]) an overall picture may be built up. The map is not time-based, but shows the shape of what is to be achieved, together with contributors and dependencies. The intensity of mapping is open to suggestion. A simple high-level chart may be compiled, complemented by lower-level charts for each of the outcomes shown, or a denser mapping may be achieved that shows clearly defined clusters of activity (such as resources, technology, legal activities). Some evidence of clustering is shown in Figure 20. For example, quality and resources appear in groups, but this map is really too high-level in order to show clusters adequately.

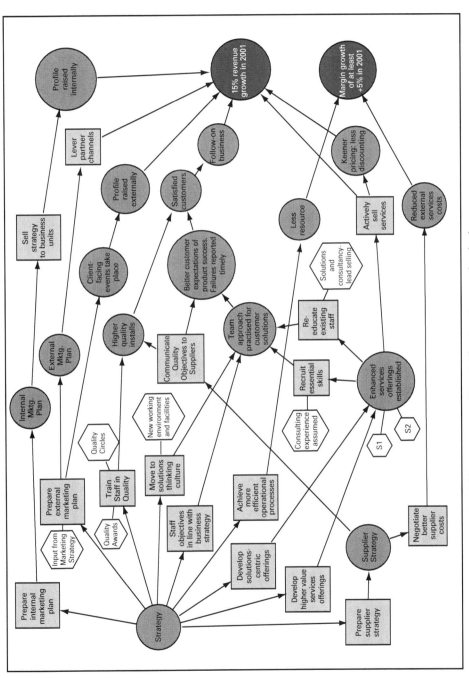

Figure 20 Example of a conceptual model for a programme blueprint for changing a services business

The strategic map is particularly useful in support of a programme blueprint, since it represents graphically the shape of the programme. It can show which pathways are stronger contributors to the end-goals. It is also possible to give an indication of the projects that need to be commissioned. Each outcome could be a single project or group of projects and change initiatives. Management responsibilities may be assigned to each outcome, with a task to produce further concept maps. A portfolio of maps may be compiled, each complementing the overall strategic map.

A good way to build the map is by group session, using large sheets of paper (A0 size) or a large whiteboard (preferably an electronic one with printer attached). Participants should feel unrestricted in their contributions. In the conceptual world there are no constraints, so the imagination can be given free rein. It is best to start with plotting the goals and gaining consensus to them. Actions to achieve the goals can then be devised. At first, there may be just actions leading directly to goals, but as a session gathers pace, participants begin to add interim initiatives and outcomes.

Root definitions

In arriving at end-goals it is important to be consistent and disciplined in the approach. Soft systems thinking advocates *root definitions*, which effectively underwrite the goals through actions. A root definition states the objective, the person or persons who need to achieve it, the person or persons to whom it applies, the means of achieving it and the environment to which it relates.

An example of a corporate goal is:

Be number one in the financial network services market by achieving a 40% market share in 2003.

A programme to implement this goal might have a root definition such as:

Devise and implement in the Customer Services Division best of breed network service offerings to blue-chip financial organisations through the acquisition of one or more global network consultancy firms and the certification of more than 60% of current network consultants.

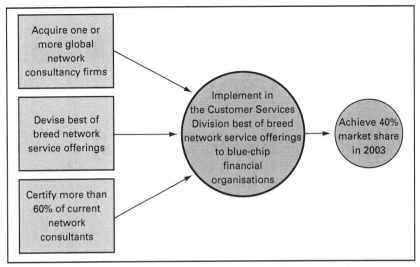

Figure 21 Using Root Definition components as a foundation for a conceptual map

One or more of the elements of this root definition might also appear in the corporate goal. In this case, the root definition shows that the company will achieve its goal partly through acquisition and certification and partly through the creation and implementation of best of breed network service offerings. The root definition interprets the work to be done. It shows that within the boundaries of the financial services market the means of achieving the goal is stated (*implementation of best of breed offerings and the acquisition of consultancy firms*). It also shows the customer for the action (*blue-chip financial organisations*), the organisation in which the work will be carried out (*Customer Services Division*) and the people who will carry out the work (*certified network consultants*). A definition of "best of breed" is desirable. Presumably, it would not be difficult for a network services firm to articulate what this should be and to quantify it.

The attractiveness of constructing root definitions to underwrite goals is that the transformation part (the means of achieving the goal) is a fast start to constructing the conceptual map. In the example above, the map would show the root definition objective *"implement in the Customer Services Division best of breed network service offerings to blue-chip financial organisations"* with three action squares, each leading to it: *"Acquire one or more global network consultancy firms"*, *"achieve certification of more than 60% of current network consultants"* and *"devise best of breed network service offerings"*. The root definition objectives lead

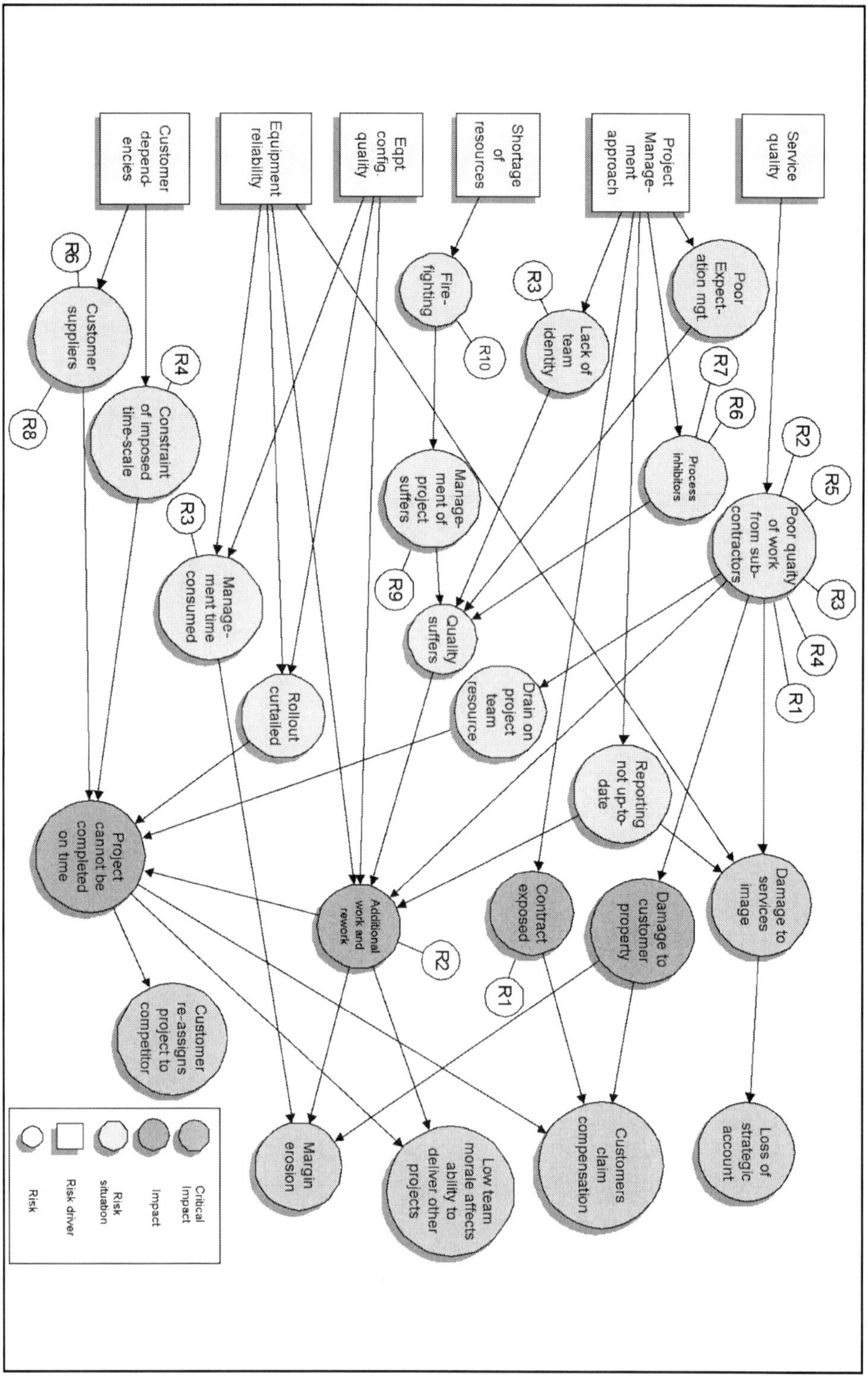

Figure 22 Example of a risk pathway from drivers to consequences

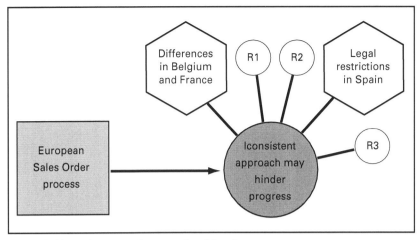

Figure 23 Alternative approach to mapping risk pathways

to the corporate goal *"achieve 40% market share in 2003"*. Figure 21 shows this graphically.

The construction of root definitions is also a good discipline. They become a sort of meta-language for stating the work to be done in a meaningful and consistent way. They can also be linked to benefits, as in the corporate goal above (*"achieve a market share of 40% in 2003"*).

Risk forecasting

Soft systems thinking can be used to good effect in forecasting the outcome of risk from cause to effect. Figure 22 shows a conceptual map of possible risk drivers leading to increasing degrees of risk outcomes or impacts. The map uses a similar symbol set to the strategic map but the symbols mean different things. The squares represent risk drivers and the circles represent either risk situations or impacts.

The risk drivers are not risks themselves but possible trigger points for risks. These lead to risk situations, which are effectively outcomes that harbour one or more risks. The risk situations can lead to other risk situations and eventually to impacts.

The map is very much an event map, since each outcome is a situation or event that can lead to an impact. Figure 22 shows risks attached to each risk situation. These risks are represented by numbers that

Figure 24 NCR's Euro Risk Room

correlate to a risk register. Depicting risks graphically enables the context of each risk to be shown. A risk register is not very good for showing dependencies.

The map is built up from left to right and is best constructed in a group session. Again, it is not time based, but represents participants' assumptions of the events that could occur in an unconstrained environment. Once a map is constructed and the level of detail decided, it may be compared to the real world. The outcomes are adjusted accordingly and additional risks may be added as they are identified. Although additional risks are added to the outcomes, the outcomes themselves tend to become stable, requiring little alteration over time. This provides a confidence that the correct picture of risk has been identified.

It is feasible to add overall probabilities to the risk outcomes. An outcome may have several risks associated with it. Each of these will have its own probability of occurrence, but an average could be calculated for the outcome itself.

A variation of this map may be constructed using hexagons to represent assumptions. Using assumptions provides more supportive information to the outcomes.

Used in conjunction with cause-and-effect diagrams, conceptual risk maps can be a useful means of showing the overall risk picture for a programme. Figure 24 shows this combination in use at NCR where I established a Risk Room for the ATM Euro Conversion Project as part of NCR's Preparation for the Euro Programme. The 12 participating countries were monitored in terms of conversion readiness, and the risk of non-compliance or hardware and software failure was calculated. Four key measures of readiness were tracked (software, support and two types of hardware) and mapped against ATM volumes and the number of customers in each country. The initial risk pathway created gave an early confidence among all parties of the scale of risk. It remained little changed throughout the project, providing a firm basis for monitoring and control.

Summary
Producing conceptual maps enables key programme-management elements to be viewed together in context. Thus goals, benefits, risk and quality can all be shown as part of an overall programme picture, rather than simply being viewed as isolated elements. All team members can visualise the contributors and dependencies for the programme, relating their own activities into the wider picture.

Conceptual mapping has the ability to gain early consensus by involving team members in interactive sessions. Constructing maps in a conceptual world allows for greater freedom of expression and fosters creativity. People generally feel more able to contribute assumptions using this method than using a linear approach. Having an overall picture or *roadmap* as a base also enables better information-sharing, since all team members can relate information directly it is received to its context.

Chapter 9

*P*rogramme
Governance

Steering a programme of business change requires particular focus. It needs an organisation structure that can allow governance and controls to operate, without being a major overhead. Chapter 4 shows how a Steering Group, Programme Director and Programme Executive fit into a typical programme organisation. These roles include a strong responsibility for direction and governance.

Governance is of no value if there is no structure to support the governance process. An early task for the Programme Executive is to agree upon a structure that will allow cyclical reporting, various types of programme and project approvals and rapid decision-making. This structure has to contain clear terms of reference and accountabilities that everyone understands. If too bureaucratic a structure is established there is a danger of decision-making bottlenecks. For example, the author has seen PRINCE-type project boards established where roles have not been well defined. This resulted in slow decision-making, since board members were seemingly unwilling to make decisions outside of monthly board meetings. The board meetings themselves became discussion shops, with ever-increasing agendas.

Whatever structure is crafted it must be documented as a programme process and communicated. Many governance processes have failed because few have understood the roles and needs of each party in a process.

Governance is not a substitution for management. It is a common mistake to misinterpret the control aspects of governance and for various governing boards to wrest control from project managers. The process of governance should create the right environment for project managers and other decision-makers within a programme, so that they are not inhibited from making day-to-day decisions.

Information types and flow

Governance is concerned with extracting just enough information from the programme to enable decisions and approvals to be made. It should not develop into an audit process or stray from a very specific remit. The information needed for governance should be built into the information reporting cycle mentioned in Chapter 5. The Programme Office will play a key role in obtaining and collating this information. Large programmes will benefit from constructing a governance scenario, which shows what information is required from various parties and for what purpose. Figure 25 gives an example. If a change structure has been established similar to Figure 6 in Chapter 3, then reporting to a Corporate PMO will be needed as well.

Whatever type of data is captured, it is important that it be consistent. The Programme Office will not want to be spending time converting data from different formats. Volume of data is another important consideration. The Steering Group, Programme Director and Programme Executive will not usually require detail, unless it is necessary to support a particular approval or an underlying problem. These governing bodies will normally require only summary-level data for governance purposes. The more consistently this is presented month on month, the better the decision-making process will be. Monthly dashboards are increasingly popular ways to present

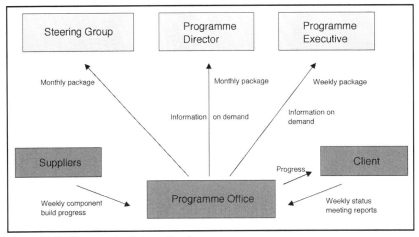

Figure 25 Outline reporting information flow

governance data, as seen in the example in Figure 26. Here reporting elements can be compared easily each month.

Common sense needs to be applied when deciding on the volume of data presented for governance purposes. In a major public-sector programme I directed, there was a contractual requirement for the client to receive detailed plans from each project on a monthly basis. This involved the rolling up and printing of almost 100,000 lines of activities each month. Quite apart from the effort of producing this material, the effort in verifying it was also substantial. Not surprisingly, the client's resources soon proved inadequate for the task of reviewing the data, and so a contract change was suggested by the client at the earliest possible convenience.

The data that is presented for governance needs to be reliable and forward-looking. In many cases, the governing bodies will expect the Programme Office to have analysed the data before it is presented, in order to show particular trends or highlight problems.

Interpretation of the data is vital. Catching problems early enough in order to tackle them effectively is a key concern for the governing bodies. Reporting only at formal stage gates is often inadequate. It is important to avoid reporting for reporting's sake. Reporting underwrites decision-making, and so must be timely, accurate and purposeful.

All those involved in the governance process must understand what data is required for what particular governance purpose. Some aspects of governance are ad hoc or singular requirements, such as the granting of approvals or the release of funds and resources. Some are tied to specific project life cycles, such as stage-gate appraisals. Some are longer-term assessments of achievement, such as the attainment of benefits. All of these require different types of data, relating to differing reporting cycles. A governance process or guidelines should make it quite clear what these requirements are and who is involved in what type of governance.

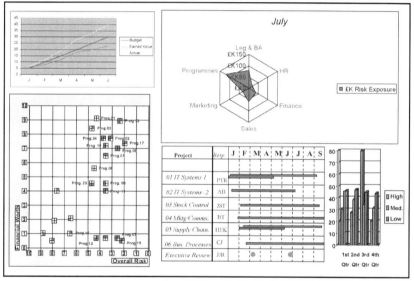

Figure 26 Sample dashboard page

Types of governance

Various types of governance may be planned for a programme of business change. A few of the more common types are reviewed below. Some governance aspects may be tied to a client contract; others may be required for internal purposes.

Progress reporting

The most common governance requirement is for the reporting of progress. Reporting may be internal or to an external client. The purpose is to provide confidence to key stakeholders that everything is proceeding to requirements, typically considering time, cost and quality.

Stakeholders also require early warning of things that are going adrift. Scope creep, duration expansions, missed milestones, schedule and cost variance are typical warning signs that governing stakeholders should consider.

Stakeholders are involved in progress governance at different levels. At the project level, each Project Manager needs regular information from the project team, suppliers and client functions in order to manage the project on a day-to-day level. Progress is usually formally reviewed at weekly progress meetings. Risks, issues, changes, milestones, resources and budget are typical of the things discussed at this level.

At the programme level, the Programme Manager and Programme Executive need progress information to manage the programme as a whole on a day-to-day level. The Steering Group (or Programme Board) and Programme Director need progress information to give direction to the programme. Their concerns are typically related to the programme scope, funding, benefits and the business strategy that the programme is executing.

Approvals and sanctions

Approvals and sanctions are also given at different levels within a programme. At the project level, a Project Manager may sanction requests within project tolerances. At a programme level, a Programme Manager may sanction requests within programme tolerances. The Steering Group may sanction requests outside of the tolerances of the programme. The difficulty arises when requests are urgent. A programme needs to allow for flexibility of approvals outside of monthly or quarterly governance sessions.

Common types of approval at a programme level are such things as resources, capital spending and subcontractor contracts. As a general rule, it is efficient to localise approvals where possible. The more approvals individual projects are allowed to make, the less burdened will the programme be. A programme that really wants to see and approve project overseas travel requests and training requirements has to understand the administrative overhead of engaging in that level of control. It is better to give the right level of tolerances and authority to lower levels, where possible.

Stage-gate appraisals

It is common for assessments to be made when projects reach particular stages or phases. Some require formal review at various stage gates, so that a project may proceed to the next gate. At a programme level, such appraisals tend to occur mainly during programme start-up, unless there are discrete phases specified, as in Table 5 in Chapter 3.

Appraisals usually result in a formal sign-off, and can be arranged around Steering Group or Project Board meetings, when relevant signatories are present.

Benefits monitoring

Benefits monitoring is a long cycle. It starts with benefits planning and ends with benefits realisation. The benefits stated in a programme's business case are the result of an often protracted period of benefits planning. By the time the business case has been signed off, the benefits as originally conceived may have been significantly diluted. There is a danger of further dilution before benefits are finally realised. This is why benefits governance is an important function for programmes and why the Business Change Manager is a key stakeholder for its successful operation. Figure 27 shows the challenge and Chapter 7 discusses the whole concept of benefits management.

The Business Change Manager monitors the achievement of benefits from the signed-off business case through to targeted realisation. The Steering Group must decide not only whether the planned achievement of benefits is sufficient to fulfil the business requirements but also whether the programme can deliver the capability to achieve them.

Benefits capability delivered by a programme's projects may be considerably less than required in the business case, as Figure 27 shows. The challenge is to redress the shortfall, but even if it is

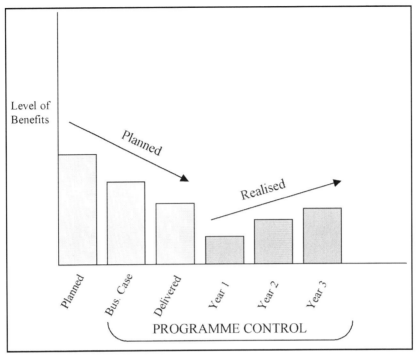

Figure 27 Benefits dilution from planned benefits to realisation

redressed, the take-up of benefits after project implementation may also fall short of expectations in the business case.

Successful benefits governance is only achievable if meaningful data can be collected from the programme and the business. Metrics need to be specified for the collection of benefits data after projects have been implemented. This presupposes that all benefits can be quantified. Tangible benefits such as revenue, cost savings and productivity may usually be tracked without too much difficulty, but intangible benefits may not be capable of being tracked.

Data collected from the planning and execution phases of projects will be varied. Variations in scope, functionality and quality will give clues to whether benefits take-up after implementation will be as planned.

Framework for governance
It will be useful to construct a framework of the governance aspects

	Governance Aspects	Strategic Alignment	Compliance	Progress	Benefits	Integrity
	Audience					
INTERNAL TO PROGRAMME SPONSOR(S)						
STEERING GROUP						
PROGRAMME EXECUTIVE						
PROGRAMME OFFICE						
PROJECTS						
EXTERNAL Customer						
Business Users						
Business Functions						
Senior Mgt						

Figure 27 Framework for governance

that the programme seeks to control. In my experience, this is best constructed with relation to the intended audience. Figure 28 shows a grid of five governance aspects in relation to an audience that is both internal and external to the programme.

The first aspect, Strategic Alignment, should be mandatory, since it enables you to record how the programme will support the business change strategy at every level. At the project level, for example, it would be essential for a project's goals to align with the goals of the strategy, via the programme. Project goals would, therefore, be a valid entry in the grid for Projects under this aspect.

The second aspect, Compliance, would be relevant where both company and external compliance is necessary to the programme. There may be many types of compliance. Technical, regulatory, external audit, contract terms and conditions, quality standards, documentation standards, health and safety, financial tolerances and security are just some of the possible compliance elements.

The third aspect, Progress, is where many of the reporting elements shown in Figure 25 can be logged. Whilst Figure 25 can show a visual summary of the reporting information flow, the framework in Figure 28 can show more detail, so is better for control purposes. Typical

Framework for Governance

	Governance Aspects	Strategic Alignment	Compliance	Progress	Benefits	Integrity
INTERNAL TO PROGRAMME						
SPONSOR(S)	Bus. Strategy Bus. Case		RAG Status	Ben. achievement	
STEERING GROUP	Bus. Strategy Bus. Case	Stage Gate approvals	RAG Status	Ben. achievement	Due diligence
PROGRAMME EXECUTIVE	Prog. Goals Prog. Charter	Sign-offs Approvals Tolerances	Monthly Dashboard	Ben. monitoring	P&L diligence Code of conduct
PROGRAMME OFFICE		Prog. standards	Progress rollup	Ben. measurement Ben. reporting	Equality compliances
PROJECTS	Project Goals Project Charter	Contract terms. Proj. standards Lessons learned	Progress reporting, TCQ	Scope & deliverable status	Supplier relations. Code of ethics Tolerances
EXTERNAL						
Customer		Acceptance criteria Handover	Progress Status	Ben. measurement Ben. monitoring	
Business Users		Operating standards	Progress Status	Ben. achievement	
Business Functions	Operational fit	Training Maintenance Support	Progress Status, as required	Payback Benefit metrics	
Senior Mgt	Operational fit	Company standards	Progress Status, as required		

TCQ = Time, Cost, Quality; P&L = Profit & Loss

Figure 29 Sample filled framework

progress elements are milestones, budget, risks, issues, changes, benefits achievement and progress against contract.

The fourth aspect, Benefits, represents more than the mere reporting of benefits that would be included under Progress. Here typical entries relate to the nature of the benefits relevant to the audience, including types of metrics and measurement processes.

The fifth aspect, Integrity, is designed to state how the programme will be managed for due diligence. Elements such as ethics, communication protocol, personnel performance, management style, negotiation protocol, supplier relations, customer relations and financial accountability are typical. Integrity is a softer form of Compliance and in some countries certain integrity elements are a legal requirement.

It is not necessary to complete every box in the grid. Indeed, it may not be possible to do so. The framework should act as a controlling summary that points to relevant detail held elsewhere. Figure 29 shows a worked example for one programme. It shows summary level information only and is not complete.

Summary

A programme, like any business operation, needs to be managed to accountability and integrity. Governance is a key consideration. The governance aspects need only be created once, then re-used for subsequent programmes. Each governance aspect needs to be considered against a relevant audience type. Clear lines of responsibility need to be defined, with supporting tolerances and authority.

In terms of collecting and reporting information the principle of "just enough" should be used. The over-collection and over-reporting of data are burdensome and inefficient. Centring information flow around an organisation chart will help all stakeholders understand the cycle of regular communication of information.

Governance and due diligence are becoming increasingly mandatory for businesses in some countries. Building a governance framework will help a programme manager maintain control and not lose sight of important elements.

Chapter 10

Conclusion

This book is a response to the need for greater structure in the management of today's types of business change, which are increasingly far-reaching and global. Programme management is a discipline well suited to this change but is best undertaken within a culture that has corporate buy-in to the management of change. There is no point implementing a company programme management method without addressing the complete corporate requirements for the management of change, though many of the techniques demonstrated in this book could be used to construct a full programme management method.

Programme management as a structured method is still evolving. There is only a handful of books published covering the complete subject. The Bibliography lists books and articles for further reading. However, the following subset may prove useful:

- *Managing Successful Programmes*; OGC; pub. TSO, London, 2007; ISBN 978-0-113-31040-1.
  The third edition of OGC's programme management framework.

- *Management of Programme Risk*; OGC; pub. TSO, London, 1995; ISBN 0 11 330672 5
  The author's account of risk in programmes, in collaboration with David La Bouchardière.
- PMI (2008), *The Standard for Programme Management*; pub. Project Management Institute, Pennsylvania, USA; ISBN 1-9781933890524
- PMI (2008), *The Standard for Portfolio Management*; pub. Project Management Institute, Pennsylvania, USA; ISBN 1-9781933890531
- *Programme Management Demystified*; Geoff Reiss; pub. Chapman Hall, 1996; ISBN: 0-419-21350-3
- *Handbook of Programme Management*; Geoff Reiss, Malcolm Anthony, John Chapman, Geof Leigh, Adrian Pyne and Paul Rayner; pub. Gower, London; ISBN 978-0-566-08603-8
- *Enterprise Programme Management – Delivering Value*; David Williams; pub. Palgrave MacMillan, 2006; ISBN: 1403917000

In the UK, the Association for Project Management (tel. +44-1494-440090) is a valuable source of information for both project and programme management. The benefits of membership are many. Its Programme Management Specific Interest Group meets to debate current techniques and experiences in the subject, and articles appear regularly in its journal Project. In the US, the Project Management Institute (PMI) provides certification for programme managers.

The independent magazine, *Project Manager Today*, features regular programme management articles, and programme management is often a focus for its well-known seminars and conferences (+44 (0) 118 932 6665).

A programme management website, sponsored by Geoff Reiss, provides useful contacts, articles, a multilingual glossary of terms and details of the UK Programme Management Special Interest Group: www.e-programme.com

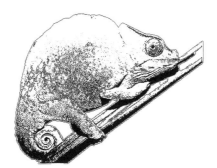

$p$rogramme Management Bibliography

Abdel-Hamid, T.K. (1993), 'A multi-project perspective of single project dynamics', *Journal of Systems & Software*, September 1993.

Archibald, Russell D. (1976), *Managing High Technology Programs And Projects*, pub. John Wiley & Sons Ltd.

Bartlett, John (1999), 'E-commerce – the next hot issue', *Project Manager Today*, September 1999.

Bartlett, John (2000), 'Managing Change as a Corporate Asset', *Proceedings of the 15th World Congress on Project Management*, June 2000 (includes Corporate Programme Office examples).

Bartlett, John (2002), 'Using Risk Concept Maps in a Project or Programme', *Proceedings of the 5th European Project Management Conference*, Cannes (PMI Europe, 2002).

Bartlett, John (2002, 2006, 2008), *Managing Risk for Projects and Programmes*, pub. Project Manager Today, 2nd edition, ISBN 978-1-900391-17-7.

Bartlett, John (2005), *Right First and Every Time: Managing Quality in Projects and Programmes*, pub. Project Manager Today, ISBN 1-900391-13-9.

Becker, Mark (1997), 'Project or Programme Management: which do Organisations need?', *Project Manager Today*, July / August 1997.

Bock, D.B.; Patterson, J.H. (1990), 'A comparison of due date setting, resource assignment and job pre-emption heuristics of the multiproject scheduling problem', *Decision Sciences*, Spring 1990.

Checkland, P.B. (1981), *Systems Thinking, Systems Practice*, pub. John Wiley, Chichester.

Cleland, David I. (1991), *Project Management – Strategic Design & Implementation*, pub. McGraw Hill.

Cooke-Davies, Terry (1994), 'Project Management and the Management of Change', *12th INTERNET World Congress on Project Management*, Oslo, Norway June 9th–11th 1994, Proceedings, Vol.1, pp. 165-169.

Coulter, C. (1990), 'Multi-project management and control', *Cost Engineering*, October 1990.

Cully, Roger (1997), 'Hector has a Smile on his Face. Do You?' (Inland Revenue Self-Assessment Programme Case Study), *Project Manager Today*, November / December 1997.

Davison, Angus (1997), 'Repackaging Projects?', *Project Manager Today*, July / August 1997.

De Maio, A; Verganti, R; Corso, M. (1994), 'A multi-project management framework for new product development', *European Journal of Operational Research*, ISSN: 0377-2217, Vol. 78, October 27 1994.

Deckro, R.F.; Winkofsky, E.P.; Hebert, J.E.; Gagnon, R. (1991), 'A decomposition approach to multi-project scheduling', *European Journal of Operational Research*, 6 March 1991.

Dumond, E.J.; Dumond, J. (1993), 'An examination of resourcing for the multi-resource problem', *International Journal of Operations and Production Management*, 13.

Ejigiri, Damien D. (1994), 'A generic framework for programme management: the cases of Robert Moses and Miles Mahoney in the US', *International Journal of Public Sector Management*, ISSN: 0951-3558, Vol: 7, Issue: 1.

Elroy, B. (1995), 'Implementing strategic change through projects', *Project – the magazine of the UK Association for Project Management*, ISSN: 0957-7033, Vol: 8, November 1995.

Eskerod, Pernille (1996), 'Meaning and action in a multi-project environment; understanding a multi-project environment by means of metaphors and basic assumptions', *International Journal of Project Management*, ISSN: 0263-7863, Vol.14, April 1996.

Fangel, Morten (1993), 'The broadening of project management', *International Journal of Project Management*, (PRM) 0263-7863, Vol: 11, Issue: 2, May 1993.

Ferns, D.C. (1991), 'Developments in programme management', *International Journal of Project Management*, August 1991.

Frumerman, Robert; Cicero, Daniel; Baetens, Charles (1987), 'R&D Programs with Multiple Related Projects', *Research Management*, ISSN: 0034-5334, Vol: 30, Issue: 5, September/October 1987.

Gareis, R. (1991), 'Management by projects: the management strategy of the "new" project-orientated company', *International Journal of Project Management*, May 1991.

Gray, Roderic (1997), 'Alternative approaches to programme management', *International Journal of Project Management*, ISSN: 0263-7863, Vol: 15, February 1997.

Harrison, J. (1993), 'BP's culture change programme', *Training & Development*, December 1993.

Hartmann, Sonke; Sprecher, Arno (1996), 'Hierarchical models for multi-project planning and scheduling', *European Journal of Operational Research*, ISSN: 0377-2217, Vol. 94, October 25 1996.

Hendricks, James A.; Bastian, Robert C.; Sexton, Thomas L. (1992), 'Bundle Monitoring of Strategic Projects', *Management Accounting*, February 1992, ISSN: 0025-1690.

Holt, Philip (1998), 'The Road to Successful Change Management Processes' (Royal Mail Case Study), *Project Manager Today*, May 1998.

Kurstedt, H.A.; Gardner, E.J.; Hindman, T.B. (1991), 'Design and use of a flat structure in a multi-project research organisation', *International Journal of Project Management*, November 1991.

Levene, R J; Braganza, A. (1996), 'Controlling the work scope in organisational transformation: a programme management approach', *International Journal of Project Management*, ISSN: 0263-7863, Vol: 14, December 1996.

Levine, H.A. (1991), 'Projects goals shifting toward enterprise goals', *Software Magazine*, December 1991.

Lonergan, K. (1994), 'Programme management', *Project – the Journal of the Association of Project Management*, July 1994.

Lonergan, K.; Dixon, M. (1994), 'Managing control systems in a programme environment', *Project – the Journal of the Association of Project Management*, October 1994.

Lord, Alexander M. (1993), 'Implementing strategy through project management', *Long Range Planning*, ISSN: 0024-6301, Vol: 26, Issue: 1, February 1993.

Mandell, Myrna P. (1994), 'Managing interdependencies through program structures: a revised paradigm', *American Review of Public Administration*, ISSN: 0275-0740, Vol: 24, Issue: 1, March 1994.

Marsh, David (1998), 'The Role of the Project and Programme Office', *Project Manager Today*, December 1997, January 1998, February 1998,

May 1999, February 2001.

McCormick, E.H.; Pratt, D.L.; Haunschild, K.B.; Hegdal, J.S. (1992), 'Staffing up for a major programme', *Civil Engineering*, January 1992.

Mumford, Alan; Honey, Peter (1986), 'Developing Skills for Matrix Management', *Industrial & Commercial Training*, ISSN: 0019-7858, Vol.18, Issue: 5, September/October 1986.

Neill, Terence V. (1994), 'The board as change masters', *Directors & Boards*, ISSN: 0364-9156, Vol: 18, Issue: 3, Spring 1994.

Nkasu, M.M. (1994), 'COMSARS: a computer-sequencing approach to multi-resource constrained scheduling', *International Journal of Project Management*, August 1994.

Nunamaker, J.F., Jr (1993), 'Automating the flow: groupware goes to work', *Corporate Computing*, March 1993.

OGC (1993a), *An Introduction to Programme Management*, TSO, ISBN: 0-11-330611-3.

OGC (1993b), *Managing Programmes of Large Scale Change*, TSO, leaflet.

OGC (1994), *Programme Management Case Studies Volume 1*, TSO, ISBN: 0-11-330666-0.

OGC (1995), *Management of Programme Risk* (John Bartlett for OGC), TSO, ISBN: 0-11-330672-5.

OGC (1995), *Programme Management Case Studies Volume 2*, TSO, ISBN: 0-11-330677-6.

OGC (2008, 3rd ed.), *Managing Successful Programmes*, TSO, ISBN: 978-0-113-31040-1.

OGC (2007, 2nd ed.), *Management of Risk: Guidance for Practitioners*, TSO, ISBN: 978-0-11-331038-8.

Padgham, Henry F. (1989), 'Choosing the Right Program Management

Organization', *Project Management Journal,* ISSN: 8756-078X, Vol: 20, Issue: 2, June 1989.

Padmaperuma, Gamini (1993), 'A K Capital project implementation system' (CPIS), *American Association of Cost Engineers Transactions,* 1993, ISSN: 0065-7158.

Palmer, B. (1994), 'Programme management in the public sector', *Project – the Journal of the Association of Project Management,* September 1994.

Palmer, B.; Reiss, G.; Gilkes, P. (1994), 'Proceedings of the programme management seminars', *Project Manager Today,* 23 March 1994.

Palmer, R. (1995), 'Practical programme management', *Project Manager Today,* January 1995.

Palmer, R. (1997), 'Avoiding that Sinking Feeling', *Project Manager Today,* July / August 1997.

Panday, K. (1994), 'No consensus on how to meet deadlines', *Management Consultancy,* July / August 1994.

Partington, D. (1996), 'The project management of organisational change', *International Journal of Project Management,* February 1996.

Payne, J.H. (1993), 'Introducing formal project management into a traditional, functionally structured organisation', *International Journal of Project Management,* November 1993.

Payne, John H. (1995), 'Management of multiple simultaneous projects: a state of the art review', *International Journal of Project Management,* ISSN: 0263-7863, Vol: 13, June 1995.

Pellegrinelli, S. (1997), 'Programme management: organising project-based change', *International Journal of Project Management,* ISSN: 0263-7863, Vol: 15, June 1997.

Platje, A.; Seidel, H. (1993), 'Breakthrough in multiproject management: how to escape the vicious circle of planning and control', *International Journal of Project Management,* November 1993.

Platje, A.; Seidel, H.; Wadman, S. (1994), 'Project and portfolio planning cycle: project-based management for the multi-project challenge', *International Journal of Project Management*, May 1994.

PMI (2008), *The Standard for Programme Management*, pub. Project Management Institute, Pennsylvania, USA, ISBN 1-9781933890524.

PMI (2008), *The Standard for Portfolio Management*, pub. Project Management Institute, Pennsylvania, USA, ISBN 1-9781933890531.

Reiss, G. (1994), 'Programme Management', parts 1 and 2, *Project Manager Today*, May and June 1994.

Reiss, G., (1996), 'Multi-Project Scheduling & Management', *IPMA'96 World Congress on Project Management*, 26 June 1996, Proceedings Vol.1, ISBN: 2-9510150-0-3.

Reiss, G., (1996), *Programme Management Demystified*, pub. Chapman Hall, ISBN: 0-419-21350-3.

Reiss, G.; Marsh, D.; Burton, D.; Curtis, P. (1994), 'The role of the programme and project office', *Project Manager Today*, 8 November 1994.

Reiss, G., (1996), 'Multi-Project Scheduling and Management', *Project – the magazine of the UK Association for Project Management*, ISSN: 0957-7033, Vol: 9, December 1996 & January 1997.

Reiss, G., (1996), 'The Delegation Model of Multi-Project Management', *IPMA'96 World Congress on Project Management*, 26 June 1996, Proceedings, Vol:1, ISBN: 2-9510150-0-3.

Reiss, G., (1997), 'Programme Planning and Control', *Project Manager Today*, July/August 1997.

Reiss, Geoff (2001), 'What does programme management mean to you?', *Project Manager Today*, May 2001.

Reiss, Geoff, Malcolm Anthony, John Chapman, Geof Leigh, Adrian Pyne and Paul Rayner, *Handbook of Programme Management*, pub.

Gower, London, ISBN 978-0-566-08603-8.

Scheinberg, M.V. (1992), 'Planning a portfolio of projects', *International Journal of Project Management*, June 1992.

Scheinberg, Mark; Stretton, Alan (1994), 'Multiproject planning. Tuning portfolio indices', *International Journal of Project Management*, ISSN: 0263-7863, Vol: 12, Issue: 2, May 1994.

Sharad, D. (1986), 'Management by Projects — An Ideological Breakthrough', *Project Management Journal*, ISSN: 0147-5363, Vol: 17, Issue: 1, March 1986.

Sipos, A. (1990), 'Multiproject scheduling', *Cost Engineering*, November 1990.

Speranza, M. Grazia; Vercellis, Carlo (1993), 'Hierarchical models for multi-project planning and scheduling', *European Journal of Operational Research*, ISSN: 0377-2217, Vol: 64, Issue: 2, January 22 1993.

Strange, Dr Glenn (1995), 'Examination of Linkage Concepts in Programme Management', *International Journal of Project Management*, ISSN: 0263-7863, Vol: 15, March, April & May 1995.

Talentino, J.; Sletten, J. (1990), 'Closing the gap: a multi-project management challenge', *Cost Engineering*, November 1990.

Tavener, I.; Hurley, D.; Innes, D. (1993), 'Resources versus projects.', *Project Manager Today*, 9 November 1993.

Thorp, John (1998), *The Information Paradox*, pub. McGraw Hill, ISBN: 0-07-134265-6.

Tsubakitani, S.; Dekro, R.F. (1990), 'A heuristic for multi-project scheduling with limited resources in the housing industry', *European Journal of Operational Research*, 6 November 1990.

Tullett, A. (1996), 'The thinking style of the managers of multiple projects', *International Journal of Project Management*, ISSN: 0263-7863, Vol: 14, October 1996.

Turner, J. Rodney; Speiser, Arnon (1992), 'Programme management and its information systems requirements', *International Journal of Project Management*, ISSN: 0263-7863, Vol: 10, Issue: 4, November 1992.

Turner, R.; Reiss, G.; Watts, M.; Meade, R. (1994), 'Programme management: the software challenge', *Project Manager Today*, 22 March 1994.

Urbaniak, Douglas F. (1991), 'Integrated Program Management Support System Is Key to Automotive Future', *Project Management Journal*, ISSN: 8756-078X, Vol: 22, Issue: 3, September 1991.

Vandersluis, Chris (1995), 'Multi-project management's conundrum', *Computing Canada*, ISSN: 0319-0161, Vol. 21, April 26 1995.

Various (2001), 'Programme management' feature in *Project Manager Today*, January 2000.

Watto, R.; Newman, P.; Brown, J. (1992), Multi-project management: tools & techniques', *Project Manager Today*, 10 March 1992.

Wilkin, David (2000), 'Profiling the "soft" benefits of programme management', *Project Manager Today,* October 2000.

Williams, David & Tim Parr, *Enterprise Programme Management – Delivering Value*, pub. Palgrave MacMillan, 2006, ISBN: 1403917000.

Williams, T.M. (1993), 'Effective project management in a matrix-management environment', *International Journal of Project Management*, February 1993.

Wilson, Brian (2000), *Systems: Concepts, Methodologies and Applications*, pub. John Wiley & Sons Ltd, ISBN: 0 471 92716 3.

Wilson, Brian (2001), *Soft Systems Methodology – Concept Model Building and Its Contribution*, pub. John Wiley & Sons Ltd.

Wirth, I. (1992), 'Project management education: current issues and future trends', *International Journal of Project Management*, February 1992.

Wirth, I.; Hibshoosh, A. (1988), 'Decision support system for multi-project scheduling of resources in blood collection programmes', *International Journal of Project Management*, November 1988.

Wootton, David (2001), 'E-business programme management', *Project Manager Today*, April 2000.

Zocher, Marc; Thompson, Gary (1992), 'Cost and Schedule Baseline Development', *American Association of Cost Engineers Transactions*, ISSN: 0065-7158, Vol: 1.

$g$lossary

Term	Meaning	Chapters
Business Case	Business and financial justification for a programme or project	3, 4
Business Change Manager	A member of the Programme Executive team focusing on expectations management, benefits management and changes to business operations.	3, **4**, 7
Business Strategy	A statement of business direction and goals.	3
Change Blueprint	Vehicles for change in support of a Business Strategy.	3, 7
Change Control	The logging and control of changes in a project or programme.	5
Change Management	The high-level management of change in a company.	1, **2**, 7

Term	Meaning	Chapters
Change Vehicle	A means to accomplish business change. A project is a change vehicle.	1, 2, 3
Design Manager	A member of the Programme Executive team responsible for the Programme Design.	4, 7
Exception	An exceptional event (risk, issue or change) in a project or programme.	5
Future Business Operation	A forecast of how a business will look after a change has been implemented.	3
Governance	The monitoring of the programme for achievement of goals, integrity, etc.	9
Issue	An immediate problem requiring resolution.	5
Programme	A collection of vehicles for change designed to achieve a strategic objective.	1
Programme Design	A discrete stage in a programme's lifespan. A detailed description of the components of a programme.	3, 4, 5, 6, 7
Programme Director	Person responsible for giving direction to the programme.	4
Programme Executive	The senior management team for a programme.	4
Programme Feasibility	A discrete stage in a programme's lifespan designed to test the viability of a programme.	3, 7
Programme Manager	Person responsible for the day-to-day management of a programme.	4

Term	Meaning	Chapters
PMO	Programme Management Office. Usually a permanent administrative and support function within a company at corporate, divisional, regional or functional level. A PMO polices and assists company change.	4, **5, 6**
Programme Office	The administrative centre for a programme	**5,** 2
Project	A vehicle for change, which is transient and has a defined start and end date.	1
Risk	A forecast of an exceptional occurrence which could become an issue.	3, **6**
Risk Exposure	A calculation of the cost of risk impacts to a project or programme.	**6**
Risk Manager	A member of the Programme Executive team responsible for the analysis and management of risk in a programme.	**4, 6**
Root definitions	A way of describing goals in the context of change.	8
Sponsor	A senior manager or executive responsible for acting as business champion for a project or programme.	**4, 6**
Steering Group	A body responsible for steering the programme.	4

*i*ndex

Topic	Page
risk analysis	91,108,109,113,114
risk management	54,64,65,71,97,98,110,111,115, 116,132
Risk Exposure	35,36,69,93,98,108-110,113-116, 167
risk forecasting	139
Risk Manager	54,60,64-66,69,91,110,111,113, 114,167
Risk Register	51,54,65,78,91,99,110,112,113 140
root definitions	134,136,137,139,167
roles	49,54,57-60,62,66,73,75,80,82, 86,87,95,103,143,144
Scope	21,22,24,25,31,32,38,39,41-44, 46,48,50-53,58,61,62,64,78,82, 86,91,101,108,116,147,149,158
Sponsor/ship	21,30,71,72,74,99,101,103,107, 108,167
Steering Group	66,71-73,84,91,143,144,147,148
subcontractors	74,91,93,94,105
success criteria	108,118,121-127
suppliers	37,49,51,62,99,101,102,105, 106,147
support	24,29,30,46,48-50,52,54,59,60, 62,68,77,78,80-83,85-88,90,94, 98,110,113,129,131,132,136, 140,141,143,144,150,152, 163-165,167
Testing	49,54,63,64,66,69,71,108-110, 113,124-126
third parties	30,67,101,103,105
timescale	21,24,26,49,51,53,98,101
tranches	53
Work elements	49,51,52
Year 2000	18,32,36,122

Project Manager Today
PUBLICATIONS

Project Manager Today Publications specialises in books and journals related to project management. Titles include:

Benefits Management – releasing project value into the business
Managing Programmes of Business Change
Managing Risk for Projects and Programmes
Managing Smaller Projects
One Project Too Many – a novel approach to the management of projects,
  portfolios and programmes
Project and Programme Accounting – a practical guide for professional
  services organisations and IT
Right First & Every Time – managing quality in projects and programmes
The Programme & Project Support Office Handbook volumes 1 & 2
Using PRINCE2 – the Project Manager's Guide

and the flagship monthly magazine:
Project Manager Today

Publishers of *Project Control Professional* on behalf of
The Association of Cost Engineers

Full details from:
Project Manager Today Publications
Unit 12, Moor Place Farm, Plough Lane, Bramshill, Hook
Hampshire RG27 0RF
Tel: 0118 932 6665
Fax: 0118 932 6663
Email: info@projectmanagertoday.co.uk
Website: www.pmtoday.co.uk

Project Manager Today also organises topical conferences and seminars.